OCT 2 3 2004

W9-BOG-106

Fyodor Dostoevsky's
CRIME AND PUNISHMENT

NOTES

A Contemporary
Literary Views Book

Edited and with an Introduction by
HAROLD BLOOM

3 5 7 9 8 6 4 2

Cover Illustration: D. A. Shmarinov; Sterling Memorial Library, Yale University

Library of Congress Cataloging-in-Publication Data

Fyodor Dostoevsky's Crime and punishment / edited and with an introduction by Harold Bloom.
p. cm – (Bloom's notes)
Includes bibliographical references and index.
Summary: Includes a brief biography of the writer, thematic and structural analysis of the work, critical views, and an index of themes and ideas.
ISBN 0-7910-4056-9
1. Dostoevsky, Fyodor, 1821–1881. Prestuplenie i nakazanie. [1. Dostoevsky, Fyodor, 1821–1881. Crime and punishment. 2. Russian literature—History and criticism.] I. Bloom, Harold. II. Series.
PG3325.P73F96 1995
891.73'3—dc20
95-45102
CIP
AC

Chelsea House Publishers
1974 Sproul Road, Suite 400
P.O. Box 914
Broomall, PA 19008-0914

Contents

User's Guide

This volume is designed to present biographical, critical, and bibliographical information on Fyodor Dostoevsky and *Crime and Punishment.* Following Harold Bloom's introduction, there appears a detailed biography of the author, discussing the major events in his life and his important literary works. Then follows a thematic and structural analysis of the work, in which significant themes, patterns, and motifs are traced. An annotated list of characters supplies brief information on the chief characters in the work.

A selection of critical extracts, derived from previously published material by leading critics, then follows. The extracts consist of statements by the author on his work, early reviews of the work, and later evaluations down to the present day. The items are arranged chronologically by date of first publication. A bibliography of Dostoevsky's writings (including both Russian texts and English translations), a list of additional books and articles on him and on *Crime and Punishment,* and an index of themes and ideas conclude the volume.

Harold Bloom is Sterling Professor of the Humanities at Yale University and Henry W. and Albert A. Berg Professor of English at the New York University Graduate School. He is the author of twenty books and the editor of more than thirty anthologies of literature and literary criticism.

Professor Bloom's works include *Shelley's Mythmaking* (1959), *The Visionary Company* (1961), *Blake's Apocalypse* (1963), *Yeats* (1970), *A Map of Misreading* (1975), *Kabbalah and Criticism* (1975), and *Agon: Towards a Theory of Revisionism* (1982). *The Anxiety of Influence* (1973) sets forth Professor Bloom's provocative theory of the literary relationships between the great writers and their predecessors. His most recent books are *The American Religion* (1992) and *The Western Canon* (1994).

Professor Bloom earned his Ph.D. from Yale University in 1955 and has served on the Yale faculty since then. He is a 1985 MacArthur Foundation Award recipient and served as the Charles Eliot Norton Professor of Poetry at Harvard University in 1987–88. He is currently the editor of the Chelsea House series Major Literary Characters and Modern Critical Views, and other Chelsea House series in literary criticism.

Introduction

Crime and Punishment, published when he was forty-five, is the first of Dostoevsky's masterpieces. It is still the best of all murder stories, with the most agile of all criminal-detective fencing matches in the relationship between Raskolnikov and Porfiry Petrovich. Porfiry, wiliest of police investigators, "attacks the criminal not with blows or proofs, but with the one really unbearable thing, uncertainty," in A. D. Nuttall's brilliant formulation. Wonderfully, Nuttall adds: "I think we may say that Dostoevsky hates Porfiry," since Porfiry is an overt utilitarian, despite his Christian rhetoric extolling the educational virtues of suffering. The police investigator's stated fondness for definite positions, his absolute security against any unlikely nihilist temptations, marks him as being utterly alien to Dostoevsky, whose fierce, obscurantist version of Christianity is a reaction-formation against the authentic nihilism that Dostoevsky shares, not so much with Raskolnikov, as with the really frightening Svidrigailov, who can be called a Shakespearean personality, akin to Iago in *Othello* and Edmund in *King Lear.* Dostoevsky feared the Iago in himself, and doubtless found even Svidrigailov more appealing than the pragmatic Porfiry.

Freedom, from all limits and restraints, supposedly is what Raskolnikov desires, and certainly Svidrigailov exemplifies such a "freedom." *Crime and Punishment* is a realistic nightmare, or apocalyptic testament, more than it is a naturalistic novel. Svidrigailov simply is the most memorable figure in the book, obscuring Raskolnikov, who after all is the protagonist, a hero-villain, and a kind of surrogate for Dostoevsky himself. Just as Iago runs off with *Othello,* and Edmund nearly steals *King Lear* (at least for me), Svidrigailov passes beyond Dostoevsky's authorial control. I think of *Crime and Punishment* and I remember first Svidrigailov's remark that he is "going to America," a moment before he pulls the trigger and kills himself. Like Edmund, Svidrigailov appeals to nature, the only goddess that either of them worships. Going to America, in this nihilistic sense, is a wholly natural matter, not only for

Svidrigailov but, I suspect, for his creator Dostoevsky as well. Svidrigailov is alienated to a much greater extent than Raskolnikov and Dostoevsky are, but differs from them more in degree than in kind. He is the end of the road upon which Raskolnikov has started out, and from which Dostoevsky had pulled himself back.

Svidrigailov belongs to what traditionally was called the Negative Sublime; he is almost as grand a negation as his models, Iago and Edmund, and as his companion Stavrogin in Dostoevsky's *The Possessed*. A negative freedom belongs to the Devil, and Svidrigailov, like Iago, is more Satanic than Milton's Satan was. Nuttall argues, very persuasively to me, that Dostoevsky had no notion of freedom except the nihilistic one, which is why Dostoevsky argued for human bondage, for a theocratic tyranny of a peculiarly inhumane kind. Raskolnikov never repudiates his murderous drive for a freedom that is power; instead he gives it up, for reasons that have no clear relation to Dostoevsky's Christian purposes in *Crime and Punishment*. Mikhail Bakhtin, the Russian master of literary theory, observed that Raskolnikov is always upon a threshold. Perhaps that is where Dostoevsky had to place him, because *Crime and Punishment* itself is a large threshold, between the abyss of nihilist freedom and the Christian space of salvation that Raskolnikov can never quite bear to enter, even if he seems to be there in the curiously dispirited "Epilogue" to the novel. ✤

Biography of
Fyodor Dostoevsky

Fyodor Mikhailovich Dostoevsky was born in Moscow on November 11 (October 30, old style), 1821. His father, a doctor at a charity hospital, sent him to a good boarding school in Moscow and then to the Army Engineering College in St. Petersburg. Dostoevsky, whose parents died while he was away at school, was unhappy in the military institution but was compelled to join the Army Engineering Corps as a draftsman in 1843. An ardent lover of literature from an early age, he resigned from the army in 1844 to pursue a career in writing.

Dostoevsky made his literary debut in 1846, with the publication of *Poor Folk*. His engaging depiction of everyday life and sympathetic view of the underdog earned him accolades from the influential critic V. G. Belinsky, who heralded the work as the first attempt at a Russian "social novel." However, his next work, *The Double* (1846), received little appreciation despite its stunning portrait of psychosis. Between 1846 and 1848, Dostoevsky published several other short stories—including "White Nights" (1949), an emotional tale of a young dreamer, and "The Honest Thief" (1848), which contained the beginnings of an idea later developed in *Crime and Punishment*—that received a similar lackluster response.

Struggling financially and suffering from epilepsy, Dostoevsky was plagued by other setbacks as well. In 1849, he and other members of the radical socialist group he had been involved with for a few years were arrested and imprisoned. After eight months in solitary confinement, he and some others were sentenced to execution. They endured the torturous preparations for death, not being informed until they stood facing the firing squad that their sentence had been commuted to hard labor.

Toiling in a Siberian prison camp for four years, Dostoevsky remained committed to writing but otherwise changed his direction. He adopted a much more conservative philosophy, supportive of the Russian Orthodox church and the monarchy.

Toward the end of his exile, he published two short pieces, but he longed to be involved in a more influential project. After marrying a poor widow and serving time in the army, Dostoevsky returned to St. Petersburg in 1859 and two years later launched a monthly periodical, *Vremya* (Time), with his older brother. Besides espousing conservative views in his publication, he also serialized his novels *The Insulted and Injured* (1861) and *The House of the Dead* (1860–62), an evocative account of life in a Siberian prison.

The public reacted positively to the magazine, and Dostoevsky enjoyed a brief taste of success. Finally able to afford a vacation, he traveled through western Europe in the summer of 1862; in "Winter Notes on Summer Impressions," he criticized life in England and France. A year later, he left the country again when the government suppressed *Vremya,* but by January 1864, he was allowed to resume publishing the periodical under the name *Epokha* (Epoch). His novella "Notes from Underground" (1864), which foreshadowed the intellectual depth and moral searching of his later work, was serialized in the new magazine.

The periodical failed within a year as misfortune continued to haunt Dostoevsky. In April his wife perished of consumption and shortly thereafter his brother died, leaving him with a stepson and four nieces and nephews to provide for. Worried by seizures and the threat of debtors' prison, he developed a bad habit of gambling and pleaded for large advances from his publisher. To meet his publisher's deadline, he hurriedly composed the melodramatic *The Gambler* (1867) and began serializing the masterful *Crime and Punishment* (1866), his "psychological account of a crime." In 1867, he married his young stenographer and left Russia to escape his creditors.

To help pay off his debts, Dostoevsky produced two more novels. In 1868, he serialized *The Idiot,* creating an epileptic title character who cannot avert tragedy despite his Christlike qualities. *The Possessed* (also known as *The Devils*), a political novel criticizing Russian revolutionaries and suggesting religion as the only solution, followed in 1872, shortly before he returned to Russia. From 1873 to 1874, he received a steady income by editing a conservative weekly periodical. After taking time out to write *A Raw Youth* (1875; also known as *The Adolescent*), he returned to editing a monthly publication, *A Writer's Diary,* in 1876. In its pages, he printed new short stories as well as his political and social commentaries. Fervently patriotic, he garnered respect even from those who did not share his beliefs.

In 1878, he ended the journal to concentrate his energies on crafting his crowning achievement, *The Brothers Karamazov* (1880). A psychological detective story about three brothers involved in their father's murder, the novel explores questions of religion and redemption with great insight and humanity. Although he planned to write a sequel, he instead returned to *A Writer's Diary.* Dostoevsky died in St. Petersburg on February 9 (January 28, old style), 1881. ❖

Thematic and Structural Analysis

In **part one, chapter one** of *Crime and Punishment* Raskolnikov is a destitute student, walking out of his squalid room in St. Petersburg, "somewhat irresolutely." One of the two main conflicts of the novel is immediately established, Raskolnikov's internal conflict, which will continue until the last moments of the book. He also "now shrinks from every kind of contact"; the second important conflict of the novel is between Raskolnikov and the rest of humanity.

His thoughts alternate between his ability to take a certain extreme action, *"that,"* and his sense that he is "only amusing himself with fancies, children's games." He believes that he has spent the last month "babbling . . . lying in a corner for days on end." Now he finds himself to be *"rehearsing* his project," about to move from thought to action.

Raskolnikov visits a pawnbroker, a cruel and miserly old woman who exploits his poverty by forcing him to accept a tiny portion of the value of his late father's watch. He carefully observes her movements, especially where she keeps her money, and makes an appointment to bring her a silver cigarette case the next day. The stage is set for his plan. As he leaves her apartment, he is overcome with revulsion at himself, stunned by the brutality of what he is contemplating: "How could such a horrible idea enter my mind? What vileness my heart seems capable of!" In **part one, chapter two**, Raskolnikov stops at a bar, where a drunk man named Marmeladov tells him his life story. Raskolnikov learns that Marmeladov is a hopeless alcoholic whose wife and children are starving because he spends all their meager income on vodka. Their situation is so desperate that his teenage daughter, Sonya, has been forced into prostitution. Still, Marmeladov drinks. It seems that he seeks out suffering. But he believes that God will redeem all of them, including his fallen daughter. Suffering is a purifying force in this novel: Raskolnikov will suffer a great deal before he is redeemed, and Sonya's suffering—along with her religious faith—will be central to Raskolnikov's progress.

Throughout Marmeladov's tale, Raskolnikov alternates between "listening attentively" and "wishing to leave." These shifting reactions signal his internal shifts between his natural compassion and his cold intellect. Raskolnikov ends up going home with Marmeladov, where he is so moved by the scene of poverty and grief that he gives the Marmeladovs what little money he has received from the pawnbroker. On the way out, he regrets his action and wishes he could get the money back. The two parts of his dual character are struggling within him.

Part one, chapter three opens the morning after Raskolnikov has met the Marmeladovs. He has slept badly and realizes that his room is suffocating and filthy. Raskolnikov is well behind on his rent, and the servant girl, Nastasya, has stopped bringing him food; she comes upstairs to tell him that the landlady plans to go to the police about him. She also delivers a letter from his mother, Pulcheria Alexandrovna. In this letter, his mother recounts how his sister, Dunya, had gotten into difficulties while working as governess for a wealthy family in their village. Her employer, Svidrigailov, had fallen in love with her, and his wife, Marfa Petrovna, had blamed Dunya for seducing him. Then a letter from Dunya surfaced, in which she firmly rejected Svidrigailov's affections. Marfa Petrovna had subsequently worked to restore Dunya's reputation and had arranged a marriage between Dunya and a well-to-do relative of hers, Luzhin. Raskolnikov's mother writes that Luzhin revealed his intention "to take as his wife an honest girl . . . who had known poverty, because . . . a husband ought not to be under any sort of obligation to his wife and it was much better if she looked upon him as her benefactor." His mother and sister are on their way to St. Petersburg for the marriage.

In **part one, chapter four**, Raskolnikov wanders the streets considering his mother's letter. He decides that Luzhin is stingy and loathsome. Dunya seems to be sacrificing herself in the hope that Luzhin will help Raskolnikov pay for his studies and perhaps even give him a job. Raskolnikov decides that the marriage must be stopped. Her situation echoes that of Sonya Marmeladova; Raskolnikov refers to Dunya's marriage as her "consent to become his legal concubine." But he also realizes that he is in no position to stop her. As he wanders, he comes upon a girl who appears to have been drugged and raped—another exploited girl akin to Sonya and Dunya. A man is following her. Raskolnikov gets the attention of a policeman and even gives his last twenty kopecks to the girl for her cab fare home. As the policeman is trying to help the girl and Raskolnikov is moving on, Raskolnikov suddenly changes his mind and says to the astonished policeman, "What is it to you?" Referring to the predatory man nearby, he says, "Let him amuse himself!"

Part one, chapter five begins with Raskolnikov's decision to visit an old friend from school, Razumikhin. He has a positive impulse to seek some human contact but decides to go "after . . . when *that* is over and done with." Instead, he wanders into a park where he falls asleep and has a terrifying nightmare about a man beating an old mare to death. In the dream, Raskolnikov is a young boy, weeping and embracing the slain horse. When he wakes up, shaken, he recognizes the similarity between the brutal bludgeoning of the mare and the murder he is planning for the old pawnbroker. In effect, both elements of his character are portrayed in the dream: He is both the tender boy and the cruel man. For the first time, he articulates the reality of the deed: "Is it possible that I shall take an axe and strike her on the head . . . that my feet will slip in the warm, sticky blood . . ." He decides that he cannot and will not do it. But then, on the way home, he overhears a conversation in which the pawnbroker's half-witted stepsister, Lizaveta, announces the exact time the next day that the old woman will be alone.

Chapter six of part one introduces a part of Raskolnikov's theory justifying the murder. He remembers listening in on a conversation at a bar several weeks before. Two students were talking about Lizaveta, describing her as innocent and kind. Nonetheless, they said, she was routinely beaten by the old pawnbroker. One of them said that he could "kill that damned old woman and rob her without a twinge of conscience." The students decided that, in fact, killing the old woman would be a good deed because her money could be put to good use in the world, that "scores of families [would be] saved from beggary." But neither of them was actually willing to commit the murder.

Raskolnikov remembers this as he prepares to carry out the crime. He sews a strap inside his coat to hold the hatchet, wraps up a fake cigarette case with string to distract the old woman, goes to her apartment, and knocks on her door.

Part one ends with murder. While the old woman tries to untie the string on his pledge, Raskolnikov strikes her in the back of the head with the hatchet. He takes her keys and a small purse from around her neck, leaving her two crosses, and struggles with the trunks and drawers in the other room. From under her bed he steals some trinkets, the pledges of other people. He hears a sound in the other room and finds Lizaveta staring at her stepsister's body in shock and terror. Panicking, Raskolnikov kills her too. The unexpected second murder emphasizes the two competing aspects of his personality—he kills both the evil and the good. There are other pairs in this chapter as well. Soon, two men with appointments to see the pawnbroker come to the door at the same time. They quickly realize that the door is locked from the inside and worry that the old woman is in trouble. One of them runs off to summon the landlord while the other stays behind; shortly, he gets restless and follows the first man. There are two painters on a lower floor who have just run out into the yard, roughhousing. Raskolnikov manages to sneak out of the old woman's apartment, hide in the apartment the painters have left, and then leave the building, unnoticed, after the landlord and the two men climb up the stairs to check on the old woman. He returns the hatchet and goes back to his room, where he lies "in a stupor."

Part two opens with Raskolnikov in a kind of delirium. He feels that he must destroy the evidence but repeatedly falls into unconsciousness as he attempts to do so. He is wakened by Nastasya and a police officer, who tell him that he has been summoned to the police station. Raskolnikov assumes that he has been caught and decides to confess—a decision he will make and reconsider over and over again. His punishment has already begun. He is in a state of torment; he is ill, verging on insanity, and desperate to take care of the incriminating details while at the same time resolving to admit to the murders. In fact, the police suspect nothing. He has been summoned because of his overdue rent; all they want is for him to sign an IOU promising to pay his debts. Other people in the station house are discussing the old woman's murder. Their conversation, combined with the airlessness and the smell of fresh paint, overwhelms Raskolnikov. He faints.

Chapters two, three, and four of part two describe Raskolnikov's actions during his illness and delirium following the murders. He hides the trinkets and the purse under a stone in a nearby yard—without even looking in the purse or considering the cash value of what he stole. He drops in to see his old friend Razumikhin, who offers him work translating. Raskolnikov runs out of Razumikhin's apartment suddenly and wanders along the river. He ends up at home, having a series of strange dreams and hallucinations. He eventually awakens a few days later to find that Razumikhin and Nastasya have been caring for him. Thirty-five rubles are delivered to Raskolnikov from his mother, making the murder and robbery seem all the more pointless. Zossimov, a doctor who is a friend of Razumikhin, drops in and they discuss the murder case, which makes Raskolnikov frantic.

In **chapter five of part two**, Raskolnikov meets his sister's fiancé, Luzhin. Luzhin arrives at Raskolnikov's apartment and introduces himself stiffly. He indicates the building where he will lodge Dunya and Pulcheria Alexandrovna; it is an awful place, filthy and even dangerous. Raskolnikov argues with Luzhin, referring to the information in the letter from his mother. Luzhin is greatly offended, and Raskolnikov throws him out of his room.

Chapter six of part two chronicles more of Raskolnikov's wanderings about town. He stumbles into a bar and meets a man from the police station, Zametov. They have a discussion about how the murders could have been committed. Raskolnikov outlines how he would have done it and asks, "And what if it was I who killed the old woman and Lizaveta?" Zametov is horrified but decides that Raskolnikov is delirious.

Leaving the bar, Raskolnikov runs into Razumikhin. They argue; Raskolnikov attacks Razumikhin, who has been worried about him and looking for him. Raskolnikov says, "Leave me alone! For God's sake leave me alone!" He stumbles upon the house where the murders took place. "An irresistible and inexplicable desire" draws him up to the old woman's apartment. Somehow he is surprised that her body has been taken away and that the apartment is being redecorated. He compulsively rings the doorbell, annoying the workmen and drawing attention to himself.

Part two closes with the death of the drunken Marmeladov. Raskolnikov happens to be on the street when Marmeladov is run over by a carriage. He helps carry the dying man back to the Marmeladovs' apartment, where Marmeladov dies. At the apartment, Raskolnikov meets Sonya, the young prostitute, and gives Marmeladov's wife the rest of his money to help with the funeral expenses. By coincidence, Dunya's fiancé, Luzhin, is staying at the same apartment house and sees this act. Raskolnikov returns to his apartment and finds his mother and sister waiting for him.

The first three chapters of part three are dominated by Raskolnikov's interactions with his mother, Pulcheria Alexandrovna, and his sister, Dunya, and their maneuverings with Luzhin. Raskolnikov refuses to allow the marriage to take place. Razumikhin is very helpful to the women and instantly develops a deep attachment to Dunya. We learn that Marfa Petrovna, the wife of Dunya's former employer, has died. Luzhin writes a letter to Pulcheria Alexandrovna in which he takes her to task for telling Raskolnikov about his delight over Dunya's poverty. In his letter, Luzhin also implies that Raskolnikov used his mother's money to pay for the services of a prostitute, Sonya. He asks to meet with Dunya and her mother, without Raskolnikov, to discuss matters.

In **chapter four of part three**, Sonya stops by Raskolnikov's apartment to thank him for his money and to invite him to the funeral of her father, Marmeladov, which will be held the next day. She is upset when she realizes how impoverished he is and that he has given her everything he had. Also, because she is a prostitute, she is embarrassed at being seated between Raskolnikov's mother and sister. Razumikhin and Raskolnikov set out to see Porfiry Petrovich, a police investigator who is also Razumikhin's uncle.

Chapter five of part three contains the first full discussion of Raskolnikov's theory about crime. As Raskolnikov meets with Porfiry, ostensibly to report the items he had left with the old pawnbroker, his thoughts are whirling. He believes that Porfiry and Zametov (also present) are certain of his guilt and are merely trying to trip him up. Porfiry brings the conversation around to an article Raskolnikov had written several months before but was unaware had been published. Porfiry has read the article closely and summarizes its content:

> "There are persons who are able . . . who have every right to commit any wrong or crime, and that laws . . . are not made for them. . . . People are divided into two classes, the 'ordinary' and the 'extraordinary.' The ordinary ones must live in submission and have no right to transgress laws, because, you see, they are ordinary. And the extraordinary have the right to commit any crime just because they are extraordinary."

Porfiry goes on to question Raskolnikov carefully about his views, including whether he believes "literally" in the raising of Lazarus, to which Raskolnikov replies that he does. As Raskolnikov is leaving, Porfiry asks him whether he noticed any painters at the pawnbroker's apartment house the day he was there to pawn his father's watch. Raskolnikov quickly realizes that it is a trick: The painters were there only on the day of the murder. He has the presence of mind to answer correctly.

Part three closes with two ominous incidents. On the street, a man walks up beside Raskolnikov, says, "Murderer!" and walks away, leaving Raskolnikov in a state of panic. He turns his theory over in his mind and begins to feel that the old woman was not good enough or important enough to be killed in its name. The murder also makes him feel unimportant: "Oh . . . I am a louse, nothing more. . . . I myself am perhaps even worse and viler than the louse I killed."

He goes home in a state of distraction and intense worry. He has a nightmare in which the old woman laughs at him as he beats her skull with the axe. When he wakes up from this dream, Dunya's former employer, Svidrigailov, is standing in the doorway.

In **part four** Raskolnikov's own conflicting impulses become clearly embodied in two contrasting characters: Sonya personifies good—suffering, religion, passivity, and emotion; Svidrigailov personifies evil—cold intellect, selfishness, isolation, willfulness, and lust. Throughout the remainder of the book, Raskolnikov encounters the two of them alternately as he struggles with himself.

In **chapters one, two, and three of part four**, Svidrigailov, Luzhin, and Razumikhin vie for Dunya's affection. Svidrigailov indicates to Raskolnikov that Dunya's marriage to Luzhin is akin to prostitution and offers to give her ten thousand rubles so that she can avoid it. But Raskolnikov does not trust Svidrigailov and refuses to allow him to see Dunya. Luzhin tells Raskolnikov that Svidrigailov has been involved in the deaths of at least two people and is suspected of poisoning his wife. Dunya, Raskolnikov, and Luzhin have an argument in which Luzhin threatens to leave, and Dunya throws him out. Svidrigailov's wife, Marfa Petrovna, has left Dunya three thousand rubles in her will. Razumikhin proposes that they use it to start up a publishing house. As Raskolnikov is leaving, apparently for a long time, he spends a moment alone with Razumikhin during which he tells his friend to look after Dunya and her mother. Razumikhin, confused, asks why Raskolnikov is behaving so strangely. Wordlessly Raskolnikov conveys to him that he is the murderer.

Chapter four of part four contains a lengthy and pivotal discussion between Sonya and Raskolnikov. Raskolnikov goes to her apartment and intimidates and upsets her. He underscores the misery of her situation and the depth of her suffering, and he predicts that not only will her stepmother soon die of consumption, but her little sister will be forced into prostitution as well. When he has reduced her to complete despair, he bends down and kisses her foot, saying, "I prostrated myself not before you, but before all human suffering."

Their conversation turns to God. Raskolnikov torments Sonya with the idea that God does not exist, but Sonya maintains that he does. She happens to have Lizaveta's Bible (she and Lizaveta were friends). Raskolnikov insists that Sonya read to him the passage about the raising of Lazarus, in which a man who has been dead four days is resurrected by Christ—it has been four days since the murders. The implication is that perhaps Raskolnikov can be resurrected through Sonya's love and her ability to share in his suffering.

Raskolnikov tells Sonya that he knows who murdered Lizaveta and the old woman and that he will reveal the identity of the murderer the next day. Svidrigailov, who has rented a room next door, has been eavesdropping.

In **chapters five and six of part four**, Raskolnikov visits Porfiry at the police station. There the two play a game of cat and mouse. Pretending to be affable and relaxed, Porfiry keeps directing the conversation away from the case, which annoys Raskolnikov. Gradually, though, it becomes clear that Porfiry does suspect Raskolnikov of the murders. As Raskolnikov, in exasperation, insists on being either charged or released, one of the painters from the old pawnbroker's building makes a dramatic entrance—and confesses to the crime.

The first three chapters of part five involve a plot devised by Luzhin to discredit Sonya; he hopes to win back Dunya by making Sonya out to be a criminal and thus causing Dunya to question her brother's integrity. Luzhin invites Sonya to his apartment, where he is counting money. He gives her ten rubles for the funeral expenses and sends her on her way.

Later, Luzhin storms into the Marmeladov funeral dinner and accuses Sonya of stealing a hundred-ruble note from him. Sonya protests her innocence, but he produces the note from her pocket. Then a witness says that he saw Luzhin plant the note there; Raskolnikov deduces his motive, and Luzhin is forced to leave for good.

In **chapter four of part five**, Raskolnikov confesses to Sonya, in her room, that he is the murderer. Her reaction is first horror, then profound sympathy. Raskolnikov asks her, "Then you will not forsake me, Sonya?" Sonya promises that she will follow him wherever he goes, presumably to prison in Siberia.

Raskolnikov then attempts to explain his motive for the killings. He first claims it was "to rob"; then, to "make himself a Napoleon"; then again he says it was for money; then he claims that it doesn't matter anyway because the old woman was a louse; then, "I wanted to have the courage . . . I only wanted to dare!" Then he admits that he "murdered for myself, myself alone. . . . I needed to find out whether I was a louse like everyone else or a man, whether I was capable of stepping over barriers or not. Was I a trembling creature or had I the right. . . ?" Finally, he convinces himself, "I killed myself, not the old creature!"

Sonya directs him to begin atoning for his crime immediately: "Go . . . to the crossroads, first bow down and kiss the earth which you have desecrated, then bow to the whole world . . . and say aloud: 'I have done murder.' Then God will send you life again." She tries to give him her own cross to wear, and she puts on Lizaveta's, saying, "We are going to suffer together, we will bear the cross together!" He begins to accept it but then changes his mind.

Part five ends with the death of Sonya's stepmother. Raskolnikov goes home and finds Dunya waiting for him; she is convinced that he has been avoiding her and their mother because he is dogged by the false suspicion of murder. He responds simply by telling her that Razumikhin is a good man. He says good-bye to his sister, as if forever. Dunya is distraught and confused but finally leaves him alone. Svidrigailov intervenes to help Sonya pay to bury her stepmother. He also provides money so that her younger siblings will be well cared for. He reveals to Raskolnikov that he overheard his confession to Sonya and says ominously, "You shall see how easy-going I am. You shall see that it is possible to live with me."

In **chapter one of part six** Raskolnikov meets Sonya at her room, where her stepmother's body is being prayed over. She puts her head on his shoulder, even though she knows that he is a murderer. Her love makes him feel "terribly over-burdened." The next morning, Raskolnikov is visited by Razumikhin, who berates him for hurting his mother and sister. Raskolnikov "entrusts them" to Razumikhin's care. Razumikhin also announces that the painter has told in detail how he cleverly pretended to be roughhousing with his friend to better hide his guilt. They part, as if forever. Then Porfiry drops in.

In **chapter two of part six**, Porfiry reveals that he knows that the painter is innocent and that Raskolnikov himself killed the two women "for a theory." He says that he will not arrest him just yet, however: It will go easier for Raskolnikov if he confesses. Also, it seems that Porfiry wants Raskolnikov to learn a lesson, to understand for himself why the murders were wrong. Of prison Porfiry says, "Why should I put you there *in peace?*" He wants Raskolnikov to suffer because, like Sonya, Porfiry believes that suffering is the only way for Raskolnikov to be redeemed and to rejoin humanity.

Chapters three and four of part six take place largely at a restaurant where Raskolnikov speaks with Svidrigailov. On his way there, Raskolnikov is averse to seeing Sonya: "She represented an irrevocable sentence, an unchangeable resolution. He must choose between her way and his own." Conversely, he is drawn to Svidrigailov. It is as if he must resolve his connection with the dark half of his personality before he can face the suffering and redemption offered by Sonya, Porfiry, and confession.

During their conversation, Svidrigailov reveals that he raped a young girl, causing her to commit suicide, that he gambles, that he married his wife only for her money, and that he has been in debtor's prison. Raskolnikov becomes convinced that Svidrigailov is "the most shallow worthless scoundrel on the face of the earth," perhaps laying the foundation for his own imminent rejection of this aspect of his personality.

Svidrigailov details his love for Dunya, indeed his obsession with her, and his attempts to seduce her. He indicates that he is engaged to marry a fifteen-year-old girl, whose innocence and childishness excite him. He seems preoccupied, and eventually they leave the restaurant.

In **chapter five of part six**, Raskolnikov follows Svidrigailov in order to protect Dunya, but Svidrigailov convinces him that he is going somewhere else by carriage. Raskolnikov falls into deep thought and walks right past Dunya. Dunya is shocked to see him in such a state. Svidrigailov sneaks up and convinces her that he knows an important secret about her brother and that she must come to his room to discuss it. After he implies that she is childishly afraid of him, she agrees to go to his room.

There Svidrigailov tells Sonya that Raskolnikov is the murderer; he tells her about Raskolnikov's theory. She listens, becoming increasingly frantic. As she springs up to go to her brother, she realizes that the door is locked and that she has been duped. Svidrigailov begs her to love him, saying that he will save her brother if she does. In the heat of the moment, she draws a gun. He stands there, waiting for her to shoot him. She fires twice but succeeds only in nicking his head. He waits for her to reload. When she is in a position to kill him, she puts the gun down. He realizes that she will never love him and lets her go.

In **chapter six of part six**, Svidrigailov wanders around in despair. He goes home and convinces Sonya to take three thousand rubles to help Raskolnikov during his anticipated prison term. He also gives money to the family of his young fiancée, saying that he plans to go "to America," his personal code for suicide. The next morning, he shoots himself in the head, finishing the job Dunya could not do.

In **chapter seven of part six**, Raskolnikov visits his mother. He tells her that he will not see her for a long time and that he has always loved her. She is desperate to understand and help him, and he asks her to pray for him. He parts from her painfully and goes home to find Dunya waiting for him. She and Sonya have been together all day, worried that he would commit suicide. She says, "Thank God! So you still believe in life! Thank God!" He explains, "I did not believe in it, but just now, as I stood with my mother's arms round me, we both wept; I do not believe, but I have asked her to pray for me." He tells Dunya that he is going to confess, and she weeps, forgiving him. "Surely, by advancing to meet your punishment, you are half atoning your crime?" she ventures. At this he yells, "Crime? What crime? . . . Killing a foul noxious louse . . ." His struggle within still rages, although his angry, evil side speaks more and more rarely. His essential goodness begins to shine through. Dunya and Raskolnikov say good-bye to each other sadly.

Part six closes with Raskolnikov's confession to Porfiry. He first goes to see Sonya, who finally succeeds in giving him a cross to wear. He convinces Sonya that he must go to confess alone. On his way to the police station, however, he realizes that Sonya is following him and that she "would be with him always, and would follow him to the ends of the earth." He attempts to confess at the police station but loses his nerve. Outside, he sees Sonya waiting for him, and he returns to the police station. He tells the police, "It was I who killed the old woman and her sister Lizaveta with an axe . . ."

The **epilogue** is the conclusion of Raskolnikov's personal journey. He has been sentenced to only seven years in Siberia, because he confessed and because he seemed to have committed the crime in a state of madness. In Siberia, Sonya tends to him; she is beloved by all the prisoners. Raskolnikov's mother has fallen ill and died; Dunya and Razumikhin have married. Raskolnikov is not yet quite repentant. He thinks, "What makes what I have done seem to them so monstrous? . . . The fact that it was a . . . crime? What does that word mean? My conscience is easy . . ." But when Sonya becomes ill and cannot see him for several days, he begins to pine for her. She returns and he finds himself kneeling before her, weeping. At first she is alarmed, but then, "at once, in that instant, she understood and she no longer doubted that he loved her. . . . They were both pale and thin, but in their white sick faces there glowed the dawn of a new future, a perfect resurrection into a new life. Love had raised them from the dead, and the heart of each held endless springs of life for the heart of the other."

His ability to accept his suffering—his cross—has finally purified him. His theory has been shown to be utterly flawed. Once again he reads the story of Lazarus. Sonya's love, like Christ's love for Lazarus, has raised Raskolnikov from the deathlike state of his isolation, his misanthropy, and his emotionless intellectual ruminations. The mind has finally given way to the power of love; evil deeds of the past are forgiven, and Raskolnikov's bright future spreads before him. ❖

—*Catherine Park*

List of Characters

Raskolnikov, an impoverished student, is the central character of the novel. He is a complex man, sometimes compassionate and generous, sometimes indifferent and even cruel. Intellectually and emotionally isolated, he divides humanity into the "ordinary," who must live in submission and are obliged to obey the law, and the "extraordinary," who are above the law. To prove to himself that he is among the extraordinary, he murders an abusive pawnbroker. When her gentle stepsister discovers him at the scene of the crime, he also kills her. Torn by guilt but still clinging to the notion that he is above the law, he repeatedly talks himself into, then out of, confessing. When he does confess, he is sentenced to seven years in prison. There, through acceptance of his suffering and through the healing power of love, he is finally redeemed.

Marmeladov, an alcoholic whom Raskolnikov meets in a bar, has drunk his family into poverty. When he is run over and killed by a carriage, Raskolnikov meets his daughter Sonya.

Sonya, Marmeladov's eldest daughter, has been forced into prostitution to support her father, stepmother, and three siblings. Despite the suffering she endures, her religious faith remains unshaken. When Raskolnikov confesses to her, she pledges to take up his cross with him. She follows him to prison in Siberia, where, through her steadfast love, she becomes the instrument of his redemption.

Pulcheria Alexandrovna, Raskolnikov's mother, is timid but principled. Though her family has fallen on hard times, she carries herself with dignity. She is intensely devoted to her two children and has made great sacrifices to pay for Raskolnikov's education.

Dunya is Raskolnikov's beautiful, intelligent, and strong-willed sister. She agrees to marry the rich but overbearing Luzhin largely to alleviate her family's poverty. But when he attempts to bully her and her mother into repudiating Raskolnikov, Dunya breaks off the engagement. She remains loyal to her brother even after she finds out that he is a murderer.

Razumikhin is Raskolnikov's dependable, decent friend. When Raskolnikov decides to confess, he entrusts Razumikhin with taking care of his mother and sister. Razumikhin falls in love with, and eventually marries, Dunya.

Luzhin, Dunya's vain and self-satisfied fiancé, is interested in marrying someone who has known poverty so she will be beholden to him. He also believes that Dunya's beauty and education will create opportunities for his social advancement. Raskolnikov's intense dislike for him causes a rift with Dunya, and Luzhin attempts to win her back by discrediting Raskolnikov. When the plan backfires, he is forced to leave.

Svidrigailov, Dunya's former employer, is a lecherous, manipulative man who, despite being engaged to a fifteen-year-old, tries to seduce Dunya. He commits suicide after realizing that Dunya will never love him.

Porfiry Petrovich is a clever police detective. Although convinced of Raskolnikov's guilt, he does not arrest him but instead pressures Raskolnikov to confess so that he will be forced to confront his crime. ✤

Above translations are Jessie Coulson's

Critical Views

[John Lomas was a British literary critic who wrote one of the earliest articles in English on Dostoevsky. In this extract from that article, Lomas testifies to the psychological power of *Crime and Punishment* and focuses on its central characters, Raskolnikov and Sonya.]

In 1866, and in the very hour of his third defeat at the hands of fortune, appeared *Crime and Punishment,* beyond all question the finest of his works, and forming, with *Poor Folk* and *A Region of the Dead,* a trilogy of which any writer or age might feel justly proud. Here, at least, there is a definite and coherent narrative: so coherent, in fact, and so subtle in its coherence, that not a word, hardly a gesture, certainly no minutest circumstance can be left unmarked without weakening the effect of the whole. But far transcending any dramatic interest—exciting as this is, and well-sustained until almost the last page—is the value of the narrative from a psychological point of view. I know that there may be serious objection taken to such an estimate, and that the work has conduced in Russia to the spread of Nihilistic doctrine, and even to the committal of absolute crime; but it seems to me that the fault lies with the disordered intellect of a few of Dostoïewsky's readers, and that he himself emphatically "wrote to cure."

The narrative is in substance simple enough. The hero is a poor student, Raskolnikow, who, as it afterwards appears, has been strongly imbued with Nihilistic notions concerning the sacredness of life and of property. He lives in idleness, like a beaten dog, in a veritable kennel of a lodging, allowing his mother and sister to suffer hardship and degradation in order that his own head may be kept just above water: possessed, moreover, of a knowledge of his latent powers, and of the grand possibilities of life, in magnificent contrast with his habits and surroundings. We find him haunted by a temptation—at first so distant and impalpable, as to be hardly a temptation— to "suppress" a wretched old female usurer, who not only lives upon such ne'er-do-weels as himself, and grows rich thereby, but makes herself generally objectionable to the world at large, and to a poor long-suffering sister in particular. "What an essentially good action it would be, after all," he thinks, "to rid society of this pest! to possess oneself (especially so gifted a self as I am) of her wealth; and thenceforth, freed from every burden, to spend one's life in benevolent purpose and action!" The scheme gradually lays irresistible hold upon him: it is cherished and matured in every detail, even while it is treated as a chimæra, and finally, through the compelling power of a chain of seemingly providential circumstances, is carried into effect. Then straightway begins the punishment. Raskolnikow is, in reality, far too noble to profit in any way by his sin: he becomes the prey, not exactly of remorse—as we understand the feeling—but of an unrestful, isolating, disappointed, self-condemnatory frame of mind analogous thereto; and in the end, after playing with the justice which has got scent of him, alternately fascinated and repelled by the notion that he must give himself up, he yields to the dictates of his repentance, and is consigned to eight years of hard labour in Siberia.

So much for the main personage in the story. There is a secondary figure, however, perhaps to some minds yet more interesting, and the more so because it is (a rare thing for Dostoïewsky!) the figure of a woman. This Sonia, Raskolnikow's unobtrusive better angel, is a young girl who, in all unspoiled delicacy and purity of mind, has made herself a common prostitute in order to support her parents. An impossible figure, it may be urged. I can only say, once more, that we are constantly bound to confess that we are in the presence of types which our English prejudices will not allow us to comprehend— among a people, strange to us, from whom we can but expect strange things. It is Sonia to whose influence Raskolnikow owes whatever noble and rational sentiments come from time to time to illuminate his perhaps exaggerated brutality: to her he owes, too, his final resurrection to a better self, and she it is who keeps close to him in his self-imposed abasement, and leaves all to accompany him in his exile. I am tempted to give an extract to show how finely the antagonism and yet mutual sympathy of these two is marked and sustained. Raskolnikow has come, in his usual aimless and desperate state of mind, into the wretched lodging where Sonia lives, and proceeds to lecture her (in terms of needless brutality) upon her foolish persistence in a hopeless course of life, and upon her want of foresight. The girl answers him, in a crushed and yet dignified way, expressing her firm trust in a God who protects the innocent. The whole of this dialogue, I may say in parenthesis, while fine in itself, is most skilfully designed to set forth in vivid colouring the degradation and wretchedness of Sonia's lot: leading up, moreover, to what would seem, without careful preparation, an absurd incident, and yet which is in reality the key-note not only of this but of nearly all Dostoïewsky's works.

—John Lomas, "Dostoïewsky and His Work," *Macmillan's Magazine* 55, No. 3 (January 1887): 196–97

❖

EDWARD GARNETT ON DOSTOEVSKY'S PROBING OF DISEASED MINDS

[Edward Garnett (1868–1937), a noted British critic and editor and the husband of Constance Garnett, an important early English translator of Dostoevsky, wrote many critical works, including *Tolstoy: His Life and Writings* (1914), *Turgenev: A Study* (1917), and *Friday Nights: Literary Criticisms and Appreciations* (1922). In this article, Garnett remarks on the neglect of Dostoevsky's work prevailing in England, attributing it to English readers' squeamish dislike of Dostoevsky's searing examination of diseased minds.]

No doubt the reason for our neglect of the great Russian author lies in the Englishman's fear of morbidity. I was delighted to find in the *Spectator* some years back a criticism on Mr. W. D. Howells's novels which defines our insular apprehensions in the naïvest fashion. "Mr. Howells," said the critic, "is a standing proof that subtlety of analysis need not involve the slightest sacrifice of wholesomeness." The sentence conjures up a comforting little picture of idyllic, wholesome surroundings, say a vicarage lawn, where the pleasant clatter of tea-things is punctuated by the vicar's voice rising sonorously amid the cries of "deuce" and "vantage" from the sunk tennis-court. Dostoievsky would be a strange and ironical guest here, nor is he in place in a London club, hotel, in any well-to-do house or suburban villa residence. There is little "wholesomeness" to be sacrificed in most of Dostoievsky's novels, but his analysis of the workings of the minds of his sick and suffering people, of the weak, the tormented, the criminal, and the possessed, show us just what value is to be placed on "wholesomeness," and how the underworld of the suffering or thwarted consciousness yields us insight into deep, dark ranges of spiritual truths for ever denied to healthy, comfortable, normal folk. Yet Dostoievsky's work demonstrates what every experienced physician knows, that no hard dividing line can be drawn between the world of health and strength and the world of disease, weakness and insanity; and that all our normal impulses and acts will shade, given the cruel pressure of circumstance, into the abnormal in an infinite, finely wrought net of deviations, all of which are, psychologically, of import. Dostoievsky's peculiar and unique value is that of the great writers he is the one who stands furthest down the slope of that deep underworld of tortuous, diseased impulse, he is the one who has established best the relation the abnormal bears to the normal mind, and the one who has most fully explored the labyrinthine workings of the mind unhinged, impaired or thrown off its balance, while still mixing with and surrounded by the world of normal men. And Dostoievsky's lifework may be likened to a long winding road, traversed by the subtlest and most deep-seeing of psychologists, who at every turn is seen questioning, listening to and commenting on the strange experiences and confessions of crowds of mental patients, some almost normal, and some insane.

⟨. . .⟩ In *Crime and Punishment* (1866), ⟨. . .⟩ though the subject is the analysis of the tortuous reasonings of a mind on the borders of delirium, first trying to justify the right to murder and then struggling with the consciousness of its guilt, the author holds with a fairly steady hand the flickering lamp by whose light we follow the intricate mental processes of the criminal's motives and acts. There is sentimentality here, and a certain love of melodramatic situation which, joined to confusion and complexity, are the defects of many of Dostoievsky's

28

pages; but these, though serious artistic blemishes, do not seri-
ously impair the force of his psychological genius.
—Edward Garnett, "A Literary Causerie: Dostoievsky,"
Academy, 1 September 1906, p. 202

❖

JANKO LAVRIN ON DOSTOEVSKY'S MORAL VALUES

[Janko Lavrin (1887–1986) was a journalist, prolific
author, and professor of Russian literature at the
University of Nottingham, England. Among his many
works are *Gogol* (1926), *Dostoevsky* (1947), and *An
Introduction to the Russian Novel* (1947). In this
extract, Lavin explores Dostoevsky's perception of
moral value and self-assertion.]

The drama of Rodion Raskolnikov is closely connected with the
chief problem of Dostoevsky, the problem of Value. A short
analysis of Raskolnikov's 'crime and punishment' may, moreover, partly explain why the two greatest modern transvaluers,
Dostoevsky and Nietzsche, arrived at precisely opposite con-
ceptions of highest individual self-assertion; for it is Raskolnikov
who presents in many respects the psychological bankruptcy of
the very basis (*i.e.,* the basis of self-will) on which Nietzsche
founded the superman.

A clear idea of Raskolnikov's mentality before his fatal deed
may be obtained from his theory of crime (set down in an article written by him long before the murder). According to that
theory, mankind is naturally divided into two categories, an
inferior and a superior. To the former belong the conservative
majority who live and must live in everlasting obedience, being
incapable of living otherwise; while in the latter are but the
exceptional men—the daring, commanding and even criminal
creators of new values. The true driving-powers of life, great
legislators, teachers, and benefactors of humanity, are found
only in the second category; and they ruthlessly destroy the
old order and break the 'sacred' laws, faithfully observed by

the community, never hesitating to sacrifice innumerable lives in the furthering of their cause. 'Not only all great men, but also all those who, by hook or by crook, have raised themselves above the common herd, men who are capable of evolving something new, must, in virtue of their innate power, be undoubtedly more or less criminals,' explains Raskolnikov to the judge Porfiry, granting them a logical and even a moral sanction for shedding blood, if this be necessary for their creative purpose.

'I am grieved to observe that the only original idea you adduce, is a *moral* right to shed blood—this opinion I find you support, even defend, with fanaticism. Moral license or authority to kill is, to my mind, even more terrible than official legal authority to the same effect,' observed his friend Razumihin.

So in theory Raskolnikov insists on the principle of self-will or will to power, based on 'natural selection.' He has himself been injured and rejected by life, just as the hero of the *Underworld*; yet unlike the latter, he wants to assert himself through an active protest and to join by any means, even by crime, his second, 'superhuman' category. His logic, or better still, his 'science and reason,' afforded him a complete sanction to overstep the conventional moral law in the name of his own individual law. Nevertheless, he wavered; he was constantly divided and split into two selves, albeit this cleavage took place, for the most part, on the subliminal plane. The dramatic antagonism between these two impulses has been vividly demonstrated by the great novelist. After having resolved to murder the old pawnbroker-woman, Raskolnikov dreams, for instance, a hideous symbolic dream in which drunken peasants beat to death a miserable old horse, and he awakes in shuddering horror at the mere contemplation of his criminal design.

'O, God! Am I to stand beating in her skull, to wade in warm blood, break open the lock and rob and tremble, blood flowing all around, and hide myself with the hatchet? O, God! is this indeed possible? What am I thinking of? I know well I could not endure that with which I have been torturing myself. I saw clearly yesterday as I went up the stairs how disgusting and mean and low it all was, and did I not run away in terror?'

He went out with burning eyes and shaking limbs, but he breathed more easily. Instead of the old oppression, he now felt peace and light. 'Lord, show me the way, that I may renounce these horrid thoughts of mine.' . . . As he gazed on the Neva and on the clear, red sunset, all his weakness vanished, the heavy load was lifted from his heart. 'Liberty! Liberty!' For the moment he was free from bedevilment. Yet, but a few steps farther he chanced to hear that the old woman would be alone in her home at a certain hour, and suddenly— he 'felt that now all liberty of action and free-will had gone, and everything was irrevocably decided.' In spite of his dread, he was driven into crime, like a mere tool of Fate. 'Going over all that happened to him during those days, minute by minute and step by step, he recalled later how each event always seemed to him evidence of the predetermination of his fate.'

As one in delirium, he murdered the 'old vermin,' together with her gentle, half-witted sister. And here begins the second act of his inner drama.

> —Janko Lavrin, *Dostoevsky and His Creation: A Psycho-Critical Study* (London: William Collins & Sons, 1920), pp. 98–102

❖

ERNEST J. SIMMONS ON SOME OF DOSTOEVSKY'S FEMALE CHARACTERS

[Ernest J. Simmons (1903–1972) was a professor of Russian literature at Cornell University and Columbia University. He wrote *Pushkin* (1937), *An Outline of Modern Russian Literature* (1943), and *Leo Tolstoy* (1946). In this extract, Simmons examines some of the female characters in *Crime and Punishment* and their relationship to the theme of power and submission.]

Dostoevsky's feminine characters of the Meek type are all of lowly origin, as though he were convinced that their special attributes would seem natural and plausible only among women close to the soil or crushed by poverty. Complete passivity exists in them to an equal degree, and they accept humbly and uncomplainingly everything that fate sends their way. The humility and submissiveness of Sonya, however, contain a more poignant and extreme quality because of her dishonourable calling, for she is the only prostitute among the Meek characters. This is why she experiences such horror when Raskolnikov declares that she is as honourable as his mother and sister.

There is an interesting bit of dialogue in the notes between Sonya and Raskolnikov which is only partially reflected in the novel. Sonya says to him: "In comfort and wealth you would not be able to see anything of the distress of people. God sends much unhappiness to him whom He loves very much and in whom He has much hope, so that he may learn and see more for himself, because the misery of people is more obvious in their unhappiness than in their happiness. Perhaps there is no God, he says to her. She wanted to reply, but suddenly she burst into tears. Why, what should I be without God?"

Here Dostoevsky places in Sonya's mouth his own doctrine of earning one's happiness by suffering, the lesson that Raskolnikov is forced to learn at the end of the novel. At first the hero calls her a "religious maniac." In truth, a large element of mysticism, subtly attuned to her meekness, is deeply rooted in her fatalistic nature. Later characters in this group reflect it to an even greater degree. Sonya is convinced that the acts of her life depend upon some mysterious, all-powerful force, and in this dependence is expressed her complete incapacity. This supernatural power, of course, is God. When Raskolnikov asks her what God does for her, she whispers, "He does everything." (Part IV, Chapter IV) She unquestioningly accepts everything He sends, whether it be good or bad. If, in His infinite wisdom, He visits her with suffering, she willingly submits for she cannot pretend to judge the ways of God. This deep faith is Sonya's only hope in life, for it always enables her to entertain the expectation of something better. As Raskolnikov divines, she believes not only in God, but in all His miracles.

The relationship between Sonya and Raskolnikov is of the utmost importance, for upon it turns the ultimate faith of both.

His intellectual pride forces him to hate everything she represents. In his amazing categories of humanity, Sonya would occupy the lowest place among those despised "ordinary people" who are born to be submissive. On the other hand, Sonya also appeals to all the finer instincts of his nature. The submissive aspects of his own dual personality lead him to see in this prostitute an embodiment of Christian love and the very image of chastity.

Their love for each other, however, is strangely evasive in all its external manifestations, but it is quite representative of similar relations between such characters in later novels. In his art Dostoevsky, like Tolstoy, realized that love is expansive only in hidden ways, and that its loftiest expression should be treated as a secret thing. The undercurrent of passion may run high in the lives of his characters, but the verbal expression of it is carefully subdued in his pages. Ordinarily, the experience of love for Dostoevsky's Doubles is a torturing, hopeless struggle between pride and submissiveness, which expresses itself through the conflicting emotions of love and hate. This was made clear in the discussion of Natasha Ikhmeneva in *The Insulted and Injured*. There is a suggestion of this contradiction in Raskolnikov, but his destiny is worked out on a much broader psychological basis. For artistic reasons Dostoevsky deliberately mutes every outward show of love between Sonya and Raskolnikov. In the hero's case a confession of love would have amounted to an act of submission foreign to the dominant pride of his nature. His authoritarian theory of greatness has no place for love; he can neither give nor receive it. In the notes Dostoevsky reminds himself of this characteristic for future development in the very first meeting of Sonya and Raskolnikov: "He descends with her at the Marmeladovs; behaves rudely so as not to give her an excuse to fall in love with him." He is soon in love with Sonya himself, but it is an affection that never shows itself by any outward demonstration; it develops imperceptibly, like a thing of the spirit, and manifests itself only in the irresistible affinity between these strange, shy beings. Throughout the notes Dostoevsky continually warns himself not to allow any expression of love on their part, which he obviously considered to be an artistic and psychological fault in this particular situation. A note such as the following is repeated in various forms: "N.B. There is not a word of love between them. This is a *sine qua non.*"

With Sonya, certainly, any active expression of love would have been contrary to the characteristic emotional features of her type. All the passive and submissive traits of the Meek characters are most clearly evinced in their relations with the opposite sex. One hesitates to call this relationship love, since the sex element is virtually negligible. The Meek woman in love is utterly devoid of passion. In love, as in nearly everything else, she is destined to play the role of the sufferer. She considers herself infinitely below the person loved, and if there is any response to her affection, her happiness is not that of satisfied desire but of gratitude. Curiously enough, if her love is not returned, it appears to make no palpable difference in her life.

As a prostitute, however, Sonya's selflessness in love surpasses that of the other Meek characters, such as Darya Shatova in *The Possessed* and Sofiya Andreevna in *A Raw Youth.* Despite Raskolnikov's crime, she feels herself immeasurably beneath him in every respect, and her love is one of utter self-abnegation. She is willing to give all and she demands absolutely nothing in return. Even in that last scene in Siberia, when their intimate future together is symbolized by Raskolnikov's acceptance of their mutual lot of salvation by suffering, Sonya's role is still that of passive submission.

From the point of view of the novelist's art, the material for the characterization of Sonya would seem to have nothing more viable in it than the stuff of a picture of "still life." It is a tribute to Dostoevsky's genius that he was able to breathe the breath of real life into this exceptional figure. If she reminds one at times of an allegorical personification of some abstract virtue in a medieval morality play, she transcends her allegorical significance by the sheer force of the novelist's art. Perhaps it would be better to say that Sonya is a kind of living universal symbol of crushed and suffering humanity that bears within itself the undying seed of joyous resurrection.

—Ernest J. Simmons, *Dostoevsky: The Making of a Novelist* (London: Oxford University Press, 1940), pp. 160–63

❖

IVAN ROE ON RASKOLNIKOV

[Ivan Roe is the author of *Shelley: The Last Phase* (1953) and *The Breath of Corruption: An Interpretation of Dostoevsky* (1946), from which the following extract is taken. Here, Roe gives an outline of the central character of *Crime and Punishment,* arguing that Raskolnikov is Dostoevsky's most fully realized portrait.]

Any preconceived ideas the reader may have about "satanism" in Dostoievsky are dispelled when he learns how to know Raskolnikov, the hero of *Crime and Punishment,* which is formally the first of a series of great novels, but which for Dostoievsky must have been part of a continuous scheme which took shape in *The Possessed* and *The Brothers Karamazov.* For one "learns how to know" the characters in Dostoievsky, even minor ones, in a special sense; he writes with an apparent profusion of detail (really a cunning selection) which brings the reader face to face with the character, and creates such an illusion of closeness that the figures in these novels are literally unforgettable. Before reading *Crime and Punishment,* the reader may know certain facts about Raskolnikov, for few people read Dostoievsky now without some preparation: the facts are that the hero is the author of a justification of crime, and that he expounds his superman philosophy by committing murder, choosing as victim a "human louse," an old woman usurer. Another, innocent, victim also falls before his axe, but the interest which his nonchalance in committing this second murder arouses is superseded by the curious duel of wits which takes place between him and the prosecutor, and by the revelation he receives from the character of a prostitute who eventually persuades him to confess his crime and—apparently—atone for it by imprisonment in Siberia.

Not a pleasant character, superficially; and one it would tax the powers of the greatest novelist to make into a "hero," or anything less than revolting. But this Raskolnikov is not a satanist. There is, paradoxically, nothing positively evil about his nature. Even in the murder scene the reader pities him more than the victim. Throughout the book we meet him in conditions of poverty, discomfort, and agony of mind; when he appears on the page the thermometer jumps a degree or two;

he brings with him fever and sickness, hunger and sorrow, but for all this we should never gladly be rid of him, for the fantasia of his mind is a universal one; we feel that we should have acted as he acted in the circumstances—if we had possessed his own directness of purpose, and his own innocence, which society calls criminality. Raskolnikov is a murderer who does not repent; he is a sophist who wishes to destroy all who do not accept his sophistry; he is a spiritual nihilist. Yet at the same time he is a gentle character, for all his heroic will he is sustained (though he may not know it) by a love for humanity which draws us to him, so that at the end, having experienced pity and terror for his plight, and gone through the catharsis, we then feel doubt for having felt kinship with a mad murderer, who was not, like the tragic heroes of ancient drama, the victim of fate, but the artificer of the circumstances which entrapped him.

The character of Raskolnikov is Dostoievsky's first full draft of the portrayal of will in a human being. There is nothing of duality in the man; though Raskolnikov outside his obsessing dream of power shows affection, friendship, and tenderness, this is no story of Jekyll and Hyde: he murders to assert an idea, and this idea is a truth formulated by a more than usually clear brain. It is this clarity of purpose, unrelated to passing fever, which adds terror to his drama. Raskolnikov is never mad in a psychiatrist's sense of the term; though a saint might consider him possessed.

—Ivan Roe, *The Breath of Corruption: An Interpretation of Dostoievsky* (London: Hutchinson, 1946), pp. 15–16

❖

CHARLES E. PASSAGE ON *CRIME AND PUNISHMENT* AND E. T. A. HOFFMANN

[Charles E. Passage (1913–1986) was a professor at Harvard University, Columbia University, and Brooklyn College. Among his works are *Friedrich Schiller* (1975) and *Character Names in Dostoevsky's Fiction* (1982). In the following extract, Passage examines the influence of E. T. A. Hoffmann's "Petersburg Tale" on *Crime and Punishment*.]

Assimilated ⟨. . .⟩ into the final composite is many a motif from Hoffmann. The whole novel, for instance, is a "Petersburg Tale" on the grand scale. The very intensity that marks scene after scene of the work suggests a Hoffmannian atmosphere, though at no point is it possible to ascertain a specific source. The intensity is surely effected in part by the use of dream sequences. Raskolnikov's horrible vision of the horse beaten to death by drunken peasants has about it a totally un-Hoffmannian ferocity, yet the artistic use of a dream to illustrate a soul-state is quite Hoffmannian. Svidrigailov's memorable nightmare is even further from the spirit of Hoffmann and at the same time still more Hoffmannian in its deceptive interpenetration of waking and sleep, of reality and irreality, for within his dream Svidrigailov fancies that he wakes from dreaming and therewith confronts a new set of dream illusions. Even when he is awake and about, there is a Hoffmannian quality about Svidrigailov. He comes and goes mysteriously, his past veiled in mystery, he has an air of being not entirely human, like some of the sinister old men whom Hoffmann depicted. The Coppelius of *Der Sandmann* is an example taken at random. Svidrigailov is also subject to dreams and hallucinations. He insists that his late wife has visited him three times as a ghost. Dostoevski's notebooks clearly indicate that he was modelled on two fellow prisoners in his own chain-gang of the Omsk prison, the famous Orlov and Petrov. That Svidrigailov's intense self-will derives from this source is incontrovertible, but his visions, his hallucinations, his mystery have another origin. His crime of child-rape relates him to Prince Valkovski of *The Insulted and Injured,* with whom he also shares the crime of beating a peasant to death, and to the Yulian Mastokovich of *A Christmas Tree and a Wedding.* His heart is also afflicted with many of the exasperations of the Underground Man. In short, he is a concentration of evils from all corners of Dostoevski's experience, both from life and from books. Through Valkovski, his kinship may be traced to Prince Hektor of *Kater Murr.* Through Yulian Mastakovich, the line goes back to Fermino Valies of *Datura fastuosa.* Ultimately he is a composite of traits from all of Hoffmann's Molinari-villains, who among them duplicate several of his crimes: Berthold of *Die Jesuiterkirche in G.,* who was believed to have murdered his wife and who did commit suicide; Franzesko the painter and his descendant Medardus in *Die Elixiere des Teufels,* who between them left few stones of evil unturned; Fermino Valies of *Datura fastuosa,* who tempted the adolescent girl; and Prince Hektor of *Kater Murr,* who simultaneously wooed a wife and a mistress, untroubled by the murder which he had committed. Yet, with all his crimes, Svidrigailov proves more humanly credible than Prince Valkovski. He speaks more softly, he is marked by a certain pathetically lost quality,—in spite of the author's intention of making him a veritable "tiger,"—he rants less, he has less "cosmic" intentions. His human scope makes his evil the more intense, his fierce will more terrifying.

At the opposite pole from Svidrigailov stands Sonya, the wholly passive, Madonna-like figure, who patiently watches and prays. Squarely between them is Raskolnikov. On the one hand, he sees himself mirrored, even caricatured, in the man of many evils. Each has committed murder. Each in his alienation from society and in his own way, seeks love, Svidrigailov in Dunya, Raskolnikov in Sonya. After the crisis, each comes to terms with his fate, the evil man by despair and suicide, the man mixed of evil and of good, by suffering and atonement. For if Raskolnikov partakes of the nature of Svidrigailov, he also shares Sonya's aspiration toward holiness. He is the wavering sinner placed between the saintly girl and the unredeemed villain. How like the pattern of *Die Elixiere des Teufels!* There Medardus hesitated repeatedly amid his sins, now leaning toward the unredeemed Viktorin, now leaning toward the holiness of Aurelie, who in the climactic scene is actually recognized as a saint. In the parallels of Raskolnikov's and Svidrigailov's lives and crimes lies a residue of Medardus-Viktorin Double-relationship, and in the struggle through sin toward redemption there is more than a chance reflection of Hoffmann's purpose in *his* novel of crime and atonement.

—Charles E. Passage, *Dostoevski the Adapter: A Study in Dostoevski's Use of The Tales of Hoffmann* (Chapel Hill: University of North Carolina Press, 1954), pp. 142–44

❖

[Richard Peace (b. 1933), formerly a professor of Russian literature at the University of Bristol, England, is the author of *Russian Literature and the Fictionalisation of Life* (1976) and *Chekov: A Study of the Four Major Plays* (1983). In this extract, Peace contrasts the central and singular role of Raskolnikov in *Crime and Punishment* to the work's dualistic structure.]

Crime and Punishment, in as much as it is built exclusively round one character, has all the appearance of a monolith. This is deceptive; for the fabric itself of the monolith is ordered according to a dualistic structure which informs the whole work. Dualism is both Dostoyevsky's artistic method and his polemical theme. Dualism is the 'stick with two ends' with which he belabours the radicals of the sixties; for, in Raskolnikov, Dostoyevsky has chosen one of their number who, like the heroes of Pomyalovsky's novels, believes that he can conceive a crime rationally, justify it rationally and execute it rationally. It is this emphasis on man's rationality which Dostoyevsky attacks. The underground man had claimed that man's rational faculties constitute a mere twentieth part of his whole being: the error of Raskolnikov is that he mistakes the part for the whole.

Raskolnikov forces himself to subscribe to the monistic view of human nature; he tries to believe that he is self-sufficient and self-contained, that he is capable of acting solely according to the dictates of reason with that wholeness of purpose which distinguishes the positive characters of *What is to be done?* Dostoyevsky, on the other hand, exposes the dualistic nature of his hero, reveals that there is something else in Raskolnikov's make-up which runs contrary to his rationalism and which gravely undermines it.

Raskolnikov is not the whole man he takes himself to be: he is 'split in two', as his very name suggests (cf. *raskolot'*—to split). His friend Razumikhin points this out when discussing Raskolnikov's behaviour with his mother: 'It is as though two opposing characters inside him succeed one another by turns.'

(Pt. III, Ch. 2.) The clue to the nature of these 'two opposing characters' may perhaps be found in the ideas on human nature which Raskolnikov propounds in his article on crime. Here humanity is divided into 'ordinary people' and 'extraordinary people'; the first category constituting mere human material for the ambitions of the *heroes* of the second category. This is a division of humanity into submissive and aggressive elements, in which submissiveness is equated with stupidity and aggressiveness with intelligence. In inventing this theory, Raskolnikov has merely externalised his own inner conflict between urges to self-assertion (equated with reason) and promptings towards self-effacement (equated with the nonrational). That this theory does indeed reflect an inner struggle can be seen from the fact that Raskolnikov feels compelled to make a choice, and to seek his identity either as 'a Napoleon' or 'a louse'. These two extremes represent symbolically the poles of his own divided character.

Ambivalence permeates the whole novel. On the very first page we see that Raskolnikov, as he leaves his room with thoughts of the murder of one old woman in his mind, is at the same time apprehensive of another such figure—his landlady. Thus from the very first the reader is made aware of the disharmony in Raskolnikov between a ruthless side and a meek side. This dichotomy is present in scene after scene throughout the novel. The behaviour of Raskolnikov is now self-assertive, now self-effacing; now rational, now irrational; now 'bad', now 'good', and his own ambivalence is both reflected and heightened through the characters and situations he encounters.
—Richard Peace, *Dostoevsky: An Examination of the Major Novels* (Cambridge: Cambridge University Press, 1971), pp. 34–35

❖

PIERRE R. HART ON NARRATIVE TECHNIQUE IN *CRIME AND PUNISHMENT*

[Pierre R. Hart (b. 1935) is a professor of foreign languages at the University of Baton Rouge and the author of *Andrj Belyj's Petersburg and the Myth of the City* (1969) and *G. R. Derzhavin: A Poet's Progress* (1978). In this extract, Hart examines Dostoevsky's narrative technique in *Crime and Punishment,* pointing to the critical role of the narrative voice in the portrayal of Raskolnikov.]

Dostoevskij's continued experimentation with the mode of his narration suggests a concern for form which is frequently ignored. Ranging from the epistolary form of *Poor Folk* to the multi-levelled narrative structure in *The Brothers Karamazov,* his works employ many of the variants of first and third person narration. Because of this diversity, attempts to arrive at a general definition of the narrator's function have not been totally successful. Differences in the distance separating teller and tale would appear to make a consideration of function within the confines of a single work more instructive. In the present essay, I shall attempt to demonstrate the consequences of Dostoevskij's choice of narrative stances in *Crime and Punishment.* Although unobtrusive, the narrator of this novel makes his presence felt through a variety of devices and ultimately has a pronounced effect on our perception of Raskol'nikov and his crime.

On first examination, the overwhelming sense of Raskol'nikov's presence almost totally obscures the existence of an independent narrative voice. For the greater part of the novel, events are viewed from a physical vantage point which coincides with that occupied by the hero. Furthermore, the narrator frequently serves as a neutral transmitter of Raskol'nikov's experiences. Yet the fact that there is an intermediary between fictional character and reader introduces the possibility for independent commentary. Even in those scenes where the focus is firmly fixed on Raskol'nikov, there are occasions when parenthetic remarks, subtle contradictions of the hero's impressions, or unrelated digressions signal the presence of another, active consciousness. Technically, the position enjoyed by the narrator might best be defined as that of "editorial omniscience." From this vantage point, he is able to exert a relatively high degree of control over the narration without detracting from the central importance of Raskol'nikov's personality.

In the process of planning his novel, Dostoevskij expressed particular concern over the point of view to be employed. His choice was conditioned by his explicit desire to present as his hero ". . . an educated man, a man of the new generation." From the notebooks for the novel, it is evident that several approaches were considered before the final selection. Dostoevskij's original intention was to employ the hero as a first person narrator who would relate the story in the form of a confession. Subsequently, he abandoned this plan, stating that ". . . the plot's structure is such, the story must be narrated by the author and not by the hero." In the absence of any thorough explanation of this change, we are obliged to speculate as to its motivation. At several points in his notes on the problem, Dostoevskij stressed the need for "complete frankness," even "naïveté." He may have recognized the difficulty of satisfying this demand with Raskol'nikov cast in the role of narrator. Indeed, it might be argued that the very existence of fictional tension throughout the novel depends upon Raskol'nikov's inability or refusal to analyze his position with complete objectivity, thus disqualifying him as a possible narrator.

The basic model for the narration as it emerged in the completed novel is contained in the immediately following entry: "Narration from the point of view of the author, [a] sort of invisible but omniscient being, who doesn't leave his hero for a moment." In practice, the narrator did not fully comply with this prescription, for the novel's structure required that he part from Raskol'nikov at several points. But even in such instances, his relation to other figures and events is consistent with that established in the sections dealing with the main character.

Despite the shift in the point of view, the work retains a sense of the first person narrative, an effect due to the particular combination of omniscient description and "narrated monologue" employed by the narrator. Within those scenes where Raskol'nikov's impressions are primary, there is a tendency to move from the mere report of the protagonist's observations to a more dramatic form which incorporates some of the features of colloquial speech. As the narration shifts between these modes, the identities of the narrator and Raskol'nikov tend to merge, producing a category of statements that might ultimately be attributed to either of them. In defining the narrator's function, then, we must take into account both the source of a remark and the possible modifications it has undergone in the process of transmission.

One of the narrator's primary functions is to provide information about Raskol'nikov which the hero is either unable or unwilling to admit to himself. As he makes the final arguments for and against his plan to murder, the reader is provided with an independent commentary on the hero's mental condition. Throughout the novel, Raskol'nikov will return to the question of whether he is in full possession of his senses. Seen from the narrator's standpoint, the issue is resolved from the outset: "It would have been difficult to sink to a lower ebb of disorder . . ." and further "This is what happens to *some monomaniacs* [emphasis mine] who are excessively concentrated on one thing." Within the context of this basic analysis, various aspects of Raskol'nikov's behavior can be more readily explained. Transitions between the waking state and dreams, for example, tend to be indistinct and reflect upon the fusion of fact and fantasy in Raskol'nikov's isolated world. In introducing the first of his hero's nightmares, the mare beating scene, the narrator calls attention to the importance of these experiences: "Under the unhealthy conditions, dreams frequently are distinguished by an unusual vividness and an exceptional resemblance to reality . . . Such dreams, sick dreams, are always remembered for a long time and produce a strong impression on the distraught and excited human organism." Here it is not simply the abnormal state which is stressed but also, the intensity and persistence of a particular subconscious experience which has important implications for Raskol'nikov's subsequent development.

—Pierre R. Hart, "Looking Over Raskol'nikov's Shoulder: The Narrator in *Crime and Punishment*," *Criticism* 13, No. 2 (Spring 1971): 166–69

❖

WILLIAM W. ROWE ON RECURRING THEMES IN DOSTOEVSKY

[William W. Rowe is the author of *Dostoevsky: Child and Man in His Works* (1968), *Nabokov's Deceptive World* (1971), and *Nabokov and Others: Patterns in Russian Literature* (1979). In this extract, Rowe compares the themes of murder and guilt, and remarks on some other similarities between *Crime and Punishment* and *The Brothers Karamazov*.]

Murder and suicide recur almost obsessively in Dostoevsky's works. His first and last major novels, however, seem most extensively concerned with murder and the question of guilt. Indeed, *Crime and Punishment* and *The Brothers Karamazov* are strikingly similar in many ways, as I will seek to demonstrate. Despite a basic shift in emphasis, Dostoevsky may even be seen, in numerous respects, to have come full circle in the writing of these two admittedly quite different works.

While writing *The Brothers Karamazov* Dostoevsky said (in a letter to L. V. Grigoriev dated March 27, 1878) that during the winter he completely reread *Crime and Punishment*. "More than two thirds of the novel," he claimed, struck him as "something entirely new, unfamiliar." This reading may possibly have awakened old patterns and problems; it may even have urged more satisfactory resolutions.

To begin with, we may note a similarity between the murders of the old misers, Alyona Ivanovna and Fyodor Pavlovich. Both are bashed on the head soon after 7:30 in the evening. Both victims open their doors to the murderer, who (presumably, in the case of Fyodor Pavlovich) has convinced them it is safe. After this, there is much ado in each novel about the door being left open. Money is stolen from both victims, from under Alyona Ivanovna's bed and either from under Fyodor Pavlovich's mattress or from behind his ikons. Both murders (by bashing on the head) are prefigured—Alyona's, by the mare in Raskolnikov's dream, beaten on the face; Fyodor's by Mitya's kicking him in the face. Near the time of each murder another person unexpectedly appears and is also bashed on the head until blood gushes. Lizaveta, whom Raskolnikov bashes on the head, had previously aided him (by mending his shirt) and Lizaveta's holy book (*The New Testament*) appears with him at the end of the novel when he is sent to Siberia. Grigory, whom Mitya bashes on the head, had previously aided him (in childhood—stressed at the trial) and Grigory's holy book (*Holy Sayings of Saint Isaac*) turns up in Smerdyakov's room late in the novel, when he confesses to the murder.

Of course, these parallels are not quite exact. To complete this last correspondence, the convicted and presumable murderers (Mitya and Smerdyakov) must be combined. Still, these and numerous other striking and complex parallels suggest that Dostoevsky was thinking along similar lines while creating the two novels, even though parallel situations involve quite disparate characters.

For example, the very different Alyosha and Raskolnikov are both about twenty and become engaged to marry cripples. Both are said to be composed of two opposite characters (by Rakitin; and by Razumikhin). Moreover, both Alyosha and Raskolnikov are concerned about and often try to help children; and they both envision innocent child victims as especially deserving the Kingdom of Heaven. Both young men succeed in giving money to suffering families (Alyosha conveys Katerina's; Raskolnikov, his own)—families which are themselves paralleled by suffering children, a mother who is or becomes insane, and a father who drinks from a painful awareness of his own inadequacy. Furthermore, Khokhlakova's eavesdropping on Alyosha's conversation with Lise may be seen to parallel Svidrigailov's eavesdropping on Raskolnikov's confession to Sonya. Even the big stone under which Raskolnikov conceals his stolen money and pledges may bring to mind the big stone near which Alyosha first attempts to transmit Katerina's money to Snegiryov, who tramples the money on the ground.

A further parallel suggests itself between Fyodor Pavlovich and Svidrigailov. Both are older men who seem to have sent a wife to the grave. Both display an abnormal interest in the innocence of young girls. Svidrigailov finds that the shy, innocent tears of a sixteen-year-old girl are "better than beauty"; Fyodor Pavlovich was especially enticed by the "innocent eyes" of his sixteen-year-old second wife. In fact, both men seem to view sex as one of the few important values in life. Svidrigailov stresses that a young girl's innocence is "worth something," that in depravity there is "something permanent, even based on nature." Fyodor Pavlovich emphasizes the "talent" for finding something enticing in any woman whatsoever. More specifically, Fyodor's doomed passion for Grushenka seems to parallel Svidrigailov's for Dunya. And we may note a correspondence between Fyodor's two victimized young wives and Svidrigailov's two girl victims, especially since one of these hangs herself, and the other drowns herself—and drowning is mentioned in connection with each of Fyodor's wives. Prior to their deaths, both men evince an uneasy fascination for the afterworld. Fyodor tells his idea of "devils' hooks" to Alyosha and Svidrigailov tells his idea of a "little room with spiders" to Raskolnikov. Both Fyodor and Svidrigailov, moreover, express the feeling that their ominous notions may be fair or just.

> —William W. Rowe, "*Crime and Punishment* and *The Brothers Karamazov:* Some Comparative Observations," *Russian Literature Triquarterly* No. 10 (Fall 1974): 331–33

❖

ROGER B. ANDERSON ON RASKOLNIKOV AND MURDER

[Roger B. Anderson, a professor of Russian literature at the University of Kentucky, is the author of *Dostoevsky: Myths of Duality* (1986) and *Soviet-American Relations: Understanding Differences, Avoiding Conflicts* (1988). In this extract, Anderson examines Raskolnikov's fateful step across the boundaries of normal society through murder.]

Raskol'nikov is a modern attestation to man's age-old desire for a special meaning in his life above and beyond the ordinary routine of day-to-day activity. His deepest need is to "step over" some barrier, to perceive and touch something of transcendent significance that lies on the other side. Such a need immediately puts him at odds with a modern urban society where the individual is called upon to choose his identity and behavior patterns from among the established categories offered him. Hence Raskol'nikov's difficulties with his studies, potential career, family relations, friendships, and available social philosophies. Raskol'nikov's dilemma involves two related compulsions: first, rebellion against a normative reality that would have him be a passive spectator to things as they are; second, active struggle to find some structure of higher meaning within which he can place himself and thereby define himself as meaningful. In this latter respect he is a refinement of the Underground Man's rebellious principle of "freedom at any price," the desire to alter mathematical or social equations to accommodate subjective, "unrealistic" demands.

When Raskol'nikov "steps over" the limits of his society's laws he enters another dimension of being which bears many names. Depending on the variable philosophical preferences of the reader, this dimension can be called Christian, mystical, existential, or orthodox Marxist. These labels are all valid in that each can properly adapt Raskol'nikov's experience to a system of philosophical values. But Raskol'nikov's journey into himself is such a basic fact of human experience that it underpins each of these systems and does not depend on any one of them for its meaning. It is therefore appropriate to discuss the hero in terms that are not governed or limited by any single philosophy to which his condition might have reference.

Raskol'nikov seeks to achieve a radical alternative to ordinary reality, not merely to add to that reality or adjust it in some way. His search for an alternative has its own coherence and rhythm of development; its tap root goes deep into the human personality. This radical alternative is not operative on the conscious level in Raskol'nikov, but rather, wells up on its own. From the first hint to the reader that he is preparing to commit murder, and thereby defy a basic limit of his society, he is subject to a state of mind which is dream-like, out of touch with the palpable world, distinctively "other." His higher logical faculties prove inadequate before the press of unconscious preoccupations, and he falls back on a more basic mode of thought and behavior that can appropriately be called primitive. The breakdown of his rational control is present virtually from the beginning of the novel, as evidenced by his disturbed sense of time, feverish hallucinations, lethargy, neurotic fixation on small details, dreams, inability to concentrate. Reality is distorted into an alogical mass having its own symbolic composition. Raskol'nikov comes into a unique state of being in which inchoate demands for the radical alternative consistently displace ordinary social standards in order to find expression. We perceive in Raskol'nikov a demand for psychological truth rather than objective facts.

—Roger B. Anderson, "Raskolnikov and the Myth Experience," *Slavic and East European Journal* 20, No. 1 (Spring 1976): 1–2

❖

LAUREN G. LEIGHTON ON *CRIME AND PUNISHMENT* AS DETECTIVE FICTION

[Lauren G. Leighton (b. 1934) is a professor of Russian at the University of Illinois at Chicago Circle. She is the author of *Russian Romanticism: Two Essays* (1975) and *The Esoteric Tradition in Romantic Literature* (1994). In this extract, Leighton studies *Crime and Punishment* as an early experiment in the art of detective fiction.]

Here it is worthwhile to remember that *Crime and Punishment* is not only a religious, metaphysical, psychological, sociopolitical, documentary, and Realist, but also a detective novel. Not, however, a simple Whodunit, but rather a "will-he-do-it." And not only will he do it, but, after he has done it, why did he do it? And then, will he confess? Why will he confess? Or will he commit suicide instead? And finally, should he, can he, will he seek his salvation? And meanwhile, throughout the novel, what are the relationships between crime and punishment, conscience and suffering, monomania and reason, the jeopardy and redemption of a human soul? These questions are *worked out* on the novel's metaphysical-religious-psychological levels, but they are *acted out* in its simple detective-novel plot. And they are acted out with the extravagant assistance of a variety of annoyingly obtrusive coincidences. Coincidences are so pervasive in the novel, and so deliberate, that to remove them would be as to remove key bricks in a carefully constructed edifice.

Consider, for example, the most necessary coincidences—those monstrous coincidences without which the plot would surely disintegrate. On the day before the murder Raskolnikov makes an accidental detour and arrives in Hay Market Square just in time to overhear the old pawnbroker woman's feeble-minded sister Lizaveta Ivanovna inform two shopkeepers she will not be home at exactly seven o'clock the next day. That is, Raskolnikov "had learned, he had suddenly and quite unex-pectedly learned, that the next day, at exactly seven o'clock in the evening, Lizaveta, the old woman's sister, and the only person who lived with her, would not be home, and that, con-sequently at exactly seven o'clock the old woman would be *entirely alone* in the house." On the day of the murder Raskolnikov oversleeps and is accidentally awakened by a shout in the street. He manages to get out of his room and down the stairs without being seen, only to remember he has forgotten to obtain an axe, which he promptly finds in the yardkeeper's shack. ("That piece of luck put new heart into him.") Because he is late, Raskolnikov must take a shortcut which brings him to the back door of the old woman's apart-ment building just in time to crouch down alongside a haycart entering the courtyard ("as though on purpose") and thus enter the building unseen. After he murders the old woman he acci-dentally finds the keys to her trunks around her neck with the crosses. While he is searching for the money and valuables, Lizaveta unexpectedly arrives home, enters through the door he has inadvertently left open, and is also murdered. Raskolnikov is almost caught in the apartment when one of the old woman's business associates arrives for an unscheduled appointment, but he gets out when the man and a neighbor go downstairs for help. As Raskolnikov rushes down the stairs, with the neighbors rushing up towards him, he finds a door open to a just-vacated apartment and is able to hide in the nick of time. "As though by design," the painters have just run out-side in a bout of horseplay—a coincidence that has coincidental consequences later. Raskolnikov gets out of the building, man-ages to get home and return the axe before it is missed. He has walked through crowded streets in broad evening light, murdered two women in bloody fashion, missed encounters with potential witnesses by split seconds, and returned to his room without having been seen by a single human being. He has committed the perfect crime and thus proved his terrible theory.

The next day Raskolnikov is summoned to the police station—something that has never happened before (" 'And why just today?' he thought, perplexed and worried"). While he is waiting for what turns out to be a routine matter involving money, incidentally), he overhears the police discussing the murder. As it happens, the building is being painted, the station smells like the empty apartment of the day before, and he faints, thus inadvertently associating himself with the murder in the minds of the police. A few days later Raskolnikov chances to drop into the Crystal Palace restaurant where he accidentally encounters the police clerk Zamyotov, and he uses the occasion to begin his campaign of defying the police to suspect him. A few days after this Raskolnikov sets out to the police station to confess, but is prevented from doing so when he happens on the scene where Marmeladov is run over by a carriage. Marmeladov is the drunken buffoon whom Raskolnikov chanced to meet just before the murder and with whose family he now becomes involved. At the death scene in Marmeladov's room Raskolnikov meets Sonya, the prostitute daughter who will play a large role in his life, and he also runs into Zamyotov who is shocked by the sight of Raskolnikov covered with Marmeladov's blood. We learn later that this scene is also attended by Luzhin, the man to whom Raskolnikov's sister Dunya has become engaged in order to save her brother's career, and because of whom Raskolnikov is so desperate for money that, presumably, he has committed murder to get it. Luzhin happens to have just arrived in Petersburg and it turns out that he is an old acquaintance of Lebezyatnikov, the man who figured so prominently in Marmeladov's tale of woe by having Sonya thrown out of the apartment. The next day, when Sonya visits Raskolnikov, she is seen leaving by Svidrigaylov, the other, even more vile suitor for Dunya's hand, and the person with whom, as it turns out, Raskolnikov has so many strange things in common. Svidrigaylov follows Sonya home and discovers that her room is just six steps from his own. This coincidence will enable him to eavesdrop when Raskolnikov chooses her as the first recipient of his confession.

In the meantime the police inspector Porfiry has begun his game of "moth-and-candle" with Raskolnikov. At their most important confrontation Porfiry manages to break Raskolnikov down and is on the verge of springing a surprise witness on him when the housepainter Nikolay bursts in and confesses to the murder. ("But at that moment a strange incident occurred, something so utterly unexpected and out of the ordinary that neither Raskolnikov nor Porfiry could have possibly anticipated such an ending.") As it happens, Nikolay has drawn suspicion on himself by the loud horseplay at the murder scene, he has kept a piece of jewelry Raskolnikov accidentally dropped in the empty apartment, and he is that type of person who will succumb to suspicion by confession to a crime he has not committed. Raskolnikov is again saved in the nick of time, and he even gets a coincidental bonus. The surprise witness turns out to be the mysterious stranger who accosted Raskolnikov on the street the day before and accused him of the murder. The first time Raskolnikov set out to the police station to confess, he ended up at the scene of the crime instead, and there raised a scandal. It turns out now that this event convinced the stranger that Raskolnikov was the murderer. Now, however, he is so disgusted with Porfiry's treatment of Raskolnikov that he concludes he was mistaken and apologizes, thereby revealing to Raskolnikov Porfiry's plot against him.
—Lauren G. Leighton, "The Crime and Punishment of Monstrous Coincidence," *Mosaic* 12, No. 1 (Fall 1978): 94–96

❖

WILLIAM J. LEATHERBARROW ON ETHICAL QUESTIONS IN *CRIME AND PUNISHMENT*

[William J. Leatherbarrow has written *Fedor Dostoevsky: A Reference Guide* (1990) and a study of *The Brothers Karamazov* (1992). In this extract, Leatherbarrow maintains that the one certainty in

Crime and Punishment is Raskolnikov's awareness of the immorality of his crime.]

Despite all the uncertainties upon which *Crime and Punishment* rests, one overriding certainty is sustained throughout the novel: the conviction, shared by author, reader, and hero, that the crime is in the final analysis wrong. Raskolnikov is aware of the wrongness of his behavior even before he acquires, in the Epilogue, the moral understanding of *why* it is wrong. He is aware of the wrongness of his crime even during those moments when he vigorously defends it on intellectual and utilitarian grounds, for in the end the criteria against which he measures his actions derive not from the intellect but from those deeper regions of the human soul, the existence of which had been so fervently denied by rational philosophy. For example, all Raskolnikov's attempts to justify his crime are persistently confounded by the intangible, irrational, but nonetheless incapacitating sensations of alienation which overcome him from the moment of the murder onward. Despite his conviction that it is possible to commit a murder in a calculated, conscious manner, he is immobilized by a loss of will that immediately follows the act of violence. In a similar fashion he is subsequently attacked by totally unanticipated sensations of estrangement from his family, the officials at the police station, indeed from humanity as a whole, despite the fact that his self-imposed isolation had never previously worried him.

The most serious threats to Raskolnikov's attempts to come to terms with his crime spring, however, from an area of his being and a definite set of values which he apparently has never before considered relevant or applicable to ethical problems. These values comprise Raskolnikov's esthetic sense.

Any attempt to explain Raskolnikov's reaction to his crime in terms of his esthetic responses must be prefaced by a brief discussion of Dostoevsky's own esthetic views, particularly his belief that man's esthetic and ethical values are related. In his esthetic views Dostoevsky was essentially a Platonist, firmly adhering to the concept of ideal beauty. For Plato true beauty resulted from the combination of esthetic perfection with moral perfection, purity of form with purity of purpose. Man is attracted to beauty precisely because it represents for him an ideal combining harmony, perfect form, good, and purity toward which he—imperfect, inharmonious, and impure—can strive. It was this Platonist concept of the unity of ethical and esthetic categories which led Schiller to propose the possibility of the moral transfiguration of man through his esthetic awareness, an idea which Dostoevsky inherited from his lifetime devotion to the German writer. As Robert L. Jackson remarks: "The notion of beauty and the ideal . . . migrated from Plato through medieval Christian esthetics down to the romantic esthetics of Schiller and Chateaubriand, Schelling and Hegel." But it had not migrated without opposition. Many writers of the late Romantic temperament—Byron and Lermontov, for instance—had attempted to make the case against Platonist ideal beauty by depicting an esthetically attractive evil. The figure of the Romantic hero in European literature had often presented the qualities of revolt, cynicism, and moral indifference in a positive and attractive light, combining formal elegance and style, not with a moral ideal but with moral bankruptcy. We remember in Lermontov's *Geroy nashego vremeni* [A Hero of Our Time] Vera's comment about her lover Pechorin, that "in nobody else was evil so attractive."

The idea that immoral or amoral qualities could combine with formal attractiveness to produce a satisfying esthetic experience was an idea which Dostoevsky opposed throughout his life. In the figure of the Romantic hero morally neutral qualities had acquired formal elegance, but this elegance was for Dostoevsky essentially sterile. It was purely formal and could not be confused with true beauty since it lacked the ideal moral dimension. Dostoevsky elaborated his views on many occasions, in both his critical writings and his *belles-lettres.* In his essay of 1861 "Mr.——bov and the Question of Art," he dismisses the Romantic quest for beauty in evil as an esthetic aberration, a result of the self-indulgence and moral indifference current among the Byronic Romantics:

> We have seen examples where man, having achieved the ideal of his desires and not knowing what else to aim for, being totally satiated, has fallen into a kind of anguish, has even exacerbated this anguish within himself, has sought out another ideal in life and out of extreme surfeit has not only ceased to value that which he enjoys but has even consciously turned away

from the straight path, and has fomented in himself strange, unhealthy, sharp, inharmonious, sometimes even monstrous tastes, losing measure and esthetic feeling for healthy beauty and demanding instead of it exceptions.

We see this esthetic confusion in *The Devils* in the figure of Stavrogin, himself a Byronic figure gone to seed who deliberately marries a cripple in order to excite his perverted but flagging esthetic sense. It is significant that, as Peace points out, Stavrogin's wife is an ugly echo of that ideal of classical beauty, the Madonna. The same confusion leads Dmitry Karamazov to the conclusion that there must be two kinds of beauty—ideal beauty (the beauty of the Madonna) and unhealthy beauty (the beauty of Sodom). For Dostoevsky there was no such ambiguity: beauty and the ideal went hand-in-glove. Strakhov cites Dostoevsky as saying: "Only that is moral which coincides with your feeling of beauty." And in a well-known letter to N.D. Fonvizina Dostoevsky gives Christ as an example of perfect beauty precisely because in the Classical manner Christ embodies an ethical ideal in perfect physical form. In the same letter he echoes Schiller by suggesting that the esthetic sense, as manifested in love for the beauty of Christ, provides an ethical guide which is superior to reason's conception of truth: "Moreover, if it were proved to me by somebody that Christ lay outside the truth and that the truth actually lay outside Christ, then I would rather remain with Christ than with the truth." For Dostoevsky esthetic standards are absolute and immutable: only that which is good can be beautiful.

—William J. Leatherbarrow, *Fedor Dostoevsky* (Boston: Twayne, 1981), pp. 83–85

❖

JOHN JONES ON THE NARRATIVE VOICE OF *CRIME AND PUNISHMENT*

[John Jones is the author of *Dostoevsky* (1983), from which the following extract is taken. Here, Jones examines the transition from first-person narration to third-person narration and its implications in *Crime and Punishment*.]

The question, who tells us?, recalls the most important of Dostoevsky's many changes in the course of writing *Crime and Punishment*, his switch from first-person narration—the murderer's story—to what is formally third-person but proves so supple, so volatile, that the distinction between the inside and outside of Raskolnikov's head disappears when his creator wants it to. The solution to 'He was not really afraid of any landlady' might appear to be that we have here a masked first-person avowal, and that it is simply an indication of Dostoevsky's boldness that it should be surrounded by authorial statements which are firmly outside and (so to say) on top of Raskolnikov in the classical omniscient third-person mode: for example, information about his poverty, irritable frame of mind, withdrawal from society, his 'not naturally timorous and abject' disposition. But masked first-person narrative turns out to be deflected stream of consciousness—'He was not really afraid' will only transpose into 'I'm not really afraid' flitting through his head as he passes the landlady's open kitchen door—so that the past tense collapses into the present, and we find we have put our finger on something pertinent to the novel's urgency and attack and (to borrow Andrew Forge's ugly but useful key-term for late Monet) its frontality.

That Raskolnikov is not by nature timorous is the author's assurance to his readers, dependable through nineteenth-century novelistic convention. That Raskolnikov is not really afraid is, in its latent truth and force, what he tells himself. The two narrative modes walk side by side in bold yet relaxed society, and support each other in the face of the fact that Raskolnikov is shaking in his shoes. The author knows (even if Akhsharumov has to remind him) that the natural man in his hero has been laid low by the combined psychic onset of crime and punishment. Raskolnikov knows (but leaves us to infer) that his present state of mind renders chatter on the stairs intolerable, which looks like fear of his landlady but 'really' isn't. As to state of mind, Raskolnikov lives with his own continuously but inspects it only intermittently, like the rest of us; whereas the author surveys the whole truth the whole time, so that we never find him wondering whether perhaps Raskolnikov is thinking this or perhaps he is thinking that: a fact which isolates *Crime and Punishment* among the mature novels, because elsewhere Dostoevsky loves the unsettled and unsettling narrative posture of 'perhaps', particularly with his contracting and dilating collective voice, the 'we' swept by rumour and speculation which arrives in *The House of the Dead* and reaches its full flowering in *The Possessed*.

While *Crime and Punishment*'s author (or omniscient narrator) knows the truth, he picks his moment to tell it. He bides his time. Then he moves in, for example to reveal that the young hero-murderer, once the deed was done, had a completely new experience 'of infinite loneliness and estrangement'; and that this experience 'was most agonising in that it was a sensation rather than knowledge or intellectual understanding, a direct sensation, the most painful sensation he had ever experienced in his life.' Raskolnikov could never have said that—which introduces the deeper issues involved in the switch from first-person to a nominal third-person narrative. Raskolnikov lives with his pain, but most of the time he doesn't focus on it. He rubs it absently, accosting strangers in the street, seeking out a friend and within minutes exclaiming that he wants to be by himself, watching children wistfully, accusing wellwishers of persecuting him with their kindness; until at last he explodes on the brink of confession in a terrrible universal cry: 'Oh, if only I were alone and nobody loved me, and if only I had never loved anyone!'

Of course he doesn't really want to be alone. He is still just rubbing his pain when he says that. What he *really* wants is a business of the inside and outside of his head, in this case of his 'alone' juxtaposed with the authorial 'loneliness and estrangement': a rich relationship, not a flat contradiction or dead end, a relationship which evokes and nurses a distinction established as far back as *The Double*, between false solitude ('loneliness and estrangement') and true solitude which is the obverse of true society and meaningless without it.

But occasionally, as I say, Raskolnikov contemplates the pain he lives with:

The conviction that everything, even memory, even the simple power of understanding, was deserting him, began to torture him unbearably. 'What if it is beginning already, what if my punishment is already beginning? Look, over there—I thought so!' And indeed the frayed scrappy edges he had cut off from his trousers were lying strewn on the floor, in the middle of the room for everyone to see! 'What on earth can be the matter with me?' he cried again like a man utterly lost.

And this in fact, not in theory, is how crime—the bloody evidence on the floor—and punishment—Raskolnikov's agony—intertwine in the novel. A wonderful moment. It sets one hesitating between general admiration and the attempt to give point to frontality or some such term: anything to obtain leverage on a narrative mode which sweeps up event and idea, fictional past and stream-of-consciousness present, into a single impulse of this immediacy and power.
—John Jones, *Dostoevsky* (Oxford: Clarendon Press, 1983), pp. 213–15

❖

LESLIE A. JOHNSON ON RASKOLNIKOV'S CRIME

[Leslie A. Johnson has written *The Experience of Time in* Crime and Punishment (1985), from which the following extract is taken. Here, Johnson argues that Dostoevsky's views on Raskolnikov's crime can be traced through the novel by the use of subjective time and Raskolnikov's patterns of fear.]

Raskolnikov dreams of murder out of a deep hunger for new life and renewed time, but he actually commits murder in sickening fear and trembling. The knowledge of this bitterly humiliates him, for he had already diagnosed what it meant in his published article "On Crime." He takes it as proof that he is an ordinary being, "base and talentless" after all, and so he concludes when he finally decides to turn himself in. Yet this is only the verdict of Raskolnikov's ideologically contaminated consciousness. His immediate experience of the crime indicates something else. Through the logic of this experience, Dostoevsky puts forth his own view of Raskolnikov's crime. The ontological meaning of murder can be deduced from the time consciousness correlated with fear and trembling—what may be called the subjective time of dread—as Raskolnikov moves toward and consummates the premeditated murder.

Raskolnikov first enters the novel during a conscious, if tentative, act of temporal reorientation. At the time of his last visit to Alena Ivanovna, it had only been a "fanciful dream" [mechta] to murder her. "Now," however, "a month later, he was already beginning to look at it differently [. . .] and even, somehow involuntarily, already beginning to consider it as an undertaking." Raskolnikov is easing himself into relation to a definite future end, he is displacing his criminal idea from the atemporal realm of ideological "chatter" to the temporal world of purposive action. Acordingly, on the way to pawn his watch he evaluates the impact of his conspicuous hat on some unnamed future: "they'll notice it a mile off, and remember it . . . that's the main thing, they'll remember it afterwards, and it'll be a clue." And he perceives the presence of movers clearing out the apartment across the way as an opportune temporal sign: "therefore," he deduces, "on the fourth story, on this stairway and on this landing, only the old lady's apartment will be occupied for a certain period. That's good . . . in any case."

Temporal considerations such as these are natural in the undertaking of any purposive action, and it is hardly suprising that a novel of such close psychological portraiture should detail them. Yet murder is not an ordinary purpose, and Raskolnikov soon finds that progress towards it creates a particular time problem for him. Whenever he catches himself assenting to the murder as a real future eventuality, this orientation acutely sensitizes him to the temporal structure of his existence. The terms of this durational sensitivity must now be examined, for they reveal the grave personal danger of Raskolnikov's supposedly self-redemptive project.

The opening pawn scene, at which Raskolnikov announces his redemptive intention through the symbolism of the watch, culminates in an intensely antipathetic awareness of duration.

All sorts of sordid details—Alena Ivanovna's keys, the layout of her apartment, Raskolnikov's own leading questions—bring the murderous end into physical and psychological proximity. But rather than drawing him onward, this proximity makes Raskolnikov conscious of the time he has spent in criminal pre-occupations: "Could such horror really come into my head? [. . .] And I, for a whole month . . ." Burdened by this inertia, which he experiences with all the hopelessness of someone in utter destitution, he stops off at a pub and rests a while in the detached present of tipsy euphoria.

The following day, news of Dunya's engagement provides another occasion for willing the crime, i.e., for taking up a structural relationship to the distal pole of murder. Postponing a visit to Razumikhin until "the next day after *that*," Raskolnikov, as it were, consents to the murder in retrospect, from a more distant future "when everything will already [. . .] be proceeding in a new way" (emphasis Raskolnikov's). But then, recognizing the implication of such a stance, he recoils in amazement: "After *that* [. . .] but surely *that* isn't going to be? Can it really be that that will really happen?" (emphasis Raskolnikov's). Once again, the anticipation of murder as a real future possibility sensitizes Raskolnikov to the time spent in criminal preoccupations, but now he experiences this duration more fatalistically: "It suddenly became intensely revolting to him to return home: there, in the corner, in that horrible cupboard, all of *that* had been ripening now for already more than a month" (emphasis Raskolnikov's). Marmeladov, out of a similar fatalistic awareness, also puts off going home, because there, back in his horrible room, his wife's disease is also ripening toward death. Of course, strictly speaking, this analogy is specious. The fulfillment of Katerina Ivanovna's time is by now a grim matter of nature; whereas the fulfillment of Alena Ivanovna's depends on Raskolnikov's freedom to choose and to act. Raskolnikov, however, reacts as if his choice and her end were just as ineluctable. Again he drowns his despair, this time with a stiffer drink (vodka, rather than beer), which extinguishes his consciousness altogether. Even in sleep, however, Raskolnikov cannot escape his ripening criminal purpose. It comes to fruition in his imagination, transformed into the brutal nightmare murder of the horse. The connection between this dream and his own future intention is immediately apparent to Raskolnikov. "God!", he exclaims, "can it really be?" Again, the duration of his murder-bound course overwhelms him: "Why have I been tormenting myself up till now? [. . .] yesterday I absolutely realized that I will not be able to take it [. . .] Why even up to now have I still been doubting it? [. . .] Why, why even up till now?"

What does murder signify for Raskolnikov that it should condition an awareness of duration similar in its unbearable fatalism to that of the wretched Marmeladov? According to Raskolnikov's own casuistical speculations, murder merely signifies a socially prohibited boundary of human conduct. Either the transgression of it inspires fear because the masses have been conditioned to regard it as a sin or taboo; or it inspires "aesthetic" revulsion because it violates an harmonious ideal of humanness to which they have likewise been schooled. After Raskolnikov has had his first hard look at the suffering of the Marmeladovs, he belittles himself for hesitating at these boundaries. They are only "prejudices, mere fears that have been instilled," so that in reality "there are no obstacles." The extraordinary man who realizes that such fears are social conventions—"It's all conventional, relative, only a matter of forms"—should therefore be able to murder with impunity. So Raskolnikov reasons from his Nihilist ontological premise. But after the brutal nightmare murder, he discovers that prohibited boundaries, inculcated taboos, can comfort as well as intimidate the tempted man. Repelled by his own future possibility, he takes refuge behind the aesthetic boundary which prohibits the shedding of "warm sticky blood." And immediately, this sense of an obstacle translates itself into welcome temporal relief: "he felt as if he had already shed the fearful burden which had oppressed him for so long [. . .] as if a boil on his heart, which had been coming to a head all month, had suddenly burst."

—Leslie A. Johnson, *The Experience of Time in* Crime and Punishment (Columbus, OH: Slavica Publishers, 1985), pp. 49–51

❖

F. D. REEVE ON MELVILLE AND DOSTOEVSKY

[F. D. Reeve (b. 1928), a professor of Russian at Wesleyan University, is the author of *Aleksandr Blok: Between Image and Idea* (1962), *Robert Frost in Russia* (1964), and *The Russian Novel* (1966). In this extract from his book on Melville and Dostoevsky, Reeve compares the narrative technique of the two writers and the similarities between Raskolnikov and Whitejacket.]

Psychologically, man swings between submission and control. The sea uses him harshly; men use each other worse. But "man can become used even to the hardest voyage," says Melville the narrator, as Dostoevsky has Raskolnikov in *Crime and Punishment* say, "Man's a scoundrel gets used to anything!" then reflect a moment and burst out wondering, "What if man is not actually a *scoundrel?* I mean, if the human species isn't, why then everything's just prejudices, nothing but exaggerated fears, and there are no limits, and that's how it's meant to be!"

For Melville's narrator, the wondrous obverse is the "influence of habitual sights and sounds upon the human temper," the ways in which man can bring himself into harmony with his world. Melville is under no illusion that man often does so or that all men can. The standard is set by the hero, Jack Chase the "saving genius" of the ship rounding Cape Horn, the star of the shipboard play, the man of the people. Lemsford's integrity as a poet is measured not by his shore-published chapbook but by calling Jack a man of the people in response to Jack's enthusiastic irony after Lemsford's manuscript "Songs of the Sirens" has been shot out of its hiding place in cannon No. 20. "The public is one thing, Jack," says Lemsford, "and the people, another." The people necessarily draw together in their suffering, even through the suffering that glorifies the commodore. The novelist's task is to offer a view of man and a vision of justice compatible with possibility. To do that he must reuse words to create an inverted hierarchy, much as the sailors, playing with checkers, imitate and escape from the ways the officers repress them.

Melville's favored device is some form of paronomasia, usually punning, a self-regulating process in which syntactical arrangement binds the shifts of meaning. Mistaken aloft for the cooper's ghost and nearly tumbled from the rigging, Whitejacket hurls his jacket on deck and addresses it in eighteenth-century style as if it were his double: " 'Jacket,' cried I, 'you must change your complexion! you must hie to the dyer's and be dyed, that I may live. . . . I cannot consent to die for *you,* but be dyed you must for me. You can dye many times without injury; but I cannot die without irreparable loss.' " The old-fashioned punning breaks through conventional thinking, liberates the mind from unnecessary quilting.

At the end of the narrative, Whitejacket falls from the yardarm, saves his life by separating himself from his double: "I whipped out my knife . . . and ripped my jacket straight up and down, as if I were ripping open myself. With a violent struggle I then burst out of it, and was free." The sailors who earlier thought the jacket a ghost now think it a white shark and harpoon it to the bottom. Thus are practical men ever shortsighted, required to act whether defensively or generously on information no amount of experience can show them is inadequate.

The world of the ship, like the white jacket and the sea into which it falls, is not more physical than emblematic of consciousness. Rhetorically, Melville makes point after point (a reason that his ideas, like Dostoevsky's, are readily debated), but the authenticity of perceived detail makes the structure credible. Leon Howard has documented that the comic episodes— the theatricals, the fall overboard, the beard-trimming, and so on—all were taken from James Mercier's *Life in a Man-of-War, or Scenes in Old Ironsides,* showing once again that Melville often drew his material from other men's experiences. In *White Jacket,* however, he imagines himself into those experiences in broad perspective with firsthand intimacy. For example, he digresses from Whitejacket's fall—a matter of seconds—to give us half a dozen paragraphs on perceptions connected with falling; so, when the jacket goes into the water, we go, too. That is the "real" fall, no matter what arc of relativity Whitejacket described from the foretop yard to the sea abeam the mizzenmast. The conclusions drawn from the fall show how much better a representation of the world the ship is than the islands of Mardi.

Dostoevsky acknowledges the Euclidean space of usual urban perspective, but he shapes non-Euclidean space in his actors' consciousnesses, where events presentiently occur. So does Melville: Whitejacket's past goes down with his jacket, as Ahab, going down with the whale, has become his idea of Moby-Dick.

> —F. D. Reeve, *The White Monk: An Essay on Dostoevsky and Melville* (Nashville, TN: Vanderbilt University Press, 1989), pp. 109–12

❖

GARY COX ON THE INFLUENCE OF *CRIME AND PUNISHMENT*

[Gary Cox, director of Russian studies at Southern Methodist University, has written *Tyrant and Victim in Dostoevsky* (1984) and Crime and Punishment: *A Mind to Murder* (1990), from which the following extract is taken. Here, Cox argues that *Crime and Punishment* introduced not only a new type of hero but a new type of fiction.]

Crime and Punishment represents not only a new kind of hero but a new kind of fiction. It is a detective story, to be sure (although the genre barely existed), but one that focuses on the mental life of the criminal and his duel with a redemptive prosecutor. Thus the plot structure of *Crime and Punishment* was likewise an innovation.

Dostoevsky has had extraordinary impact on the writers of the twentieth century. The cosmos is divided between Tolstoy and Dostoevsky, said Lev Shestov, and this opposition has been echoed by Isaiah Berlin among others. Generally readers tend to gravitate toward one or the other, not toward both, and writers tend to take their cue either from Tolstoy's panoramic breadth or Dostoevsky's psychological depth, not from both. E. M. Forster said it was a "prophetic" character that distinguished Dostoevsky from a writer like Tolstoy, and Isaiah Berlin quoted Greek poet Archilochus to express the difference: "the fox knows many things, but the hedgehog knows the one important thing." Tolstoy is the clever fox for Berlin, Dostoevsky the wise hedgehog. Many twentieth-century writers may be placed, stylistically or ideologically, in the Dostoevskian camp. Dostoevsky's influence on Lawrence, Sartre, Camus, and Malraux has already been mentioned. Different writers have reacted to different works. Thus, it is hard to imagine Faulkner's steamy depictions of the lives of decaying rural nobility without *The Brothers Karamazov;* the antiutopian work of Huxley, Zamiatin, and Orwell is unthinkable without "The Legend of the Grand Inquisitor"; it is difficult to envision the complex attitude toward the self in Sylvia Plath's *The Bell Jar* without *The Double* (upon which she wrote a senior honors thesis); and the philosophical parody of Yury Olesha's *Envy* or of Woody Allen's work (either his movies or his early *New Yorker* sketches) could probably not exist without *Notes from Underground.*

Anyone writing about the alienation of modern man from his fellows, anyone writing about philosophically motivated crime, the validation of the self through action, the relation of thought to action, and the justification of criminal means by utopian ends, anyone writing about any of these very contemporary topics cannot ignore the groundwork provided by Dostoevsky in *Crime and Punishment.* It is not so much a matter of the specific influence on specific works; it is an attitude toward the relation between the self and the world that any modern writer imbibes from Dostoevsky. Whether they accept that attitude or reject it, they are partially formed by the experience. Thus, J. D. Salinger, Ernest Hemingway, André Malraux, Jean-Paul Sartre, Albert Camus, Günther Grass, Jerzy Kosinski, John Fowles, Richard Wright, James Baldwin, and a host of others are in Dostoevsky's debt. These names merely begin the list of debtors. Students will come up with many more.

—Gary Cox, Crime and Punishment: *A Mind to Murder* (Boston: Twayne, 1990), pp. 11–12

❖

David McDuff on Freedom in *Crime and Punishment*

[David McDuff (b. 1945) has translated several of Dostoevsky's works, including *Poor Folk and Other Stories* (1988) and *Crime and Punishment* (1991). In this extract, McDuff explores the idea of freedom in *Crime and Punishment* and argues further that Raskolnikov is not an outsider but an everyman.]

Dostoyevsky is the defender of freedom. Consequently he exhorts man to take suffering upon himself as an inevitable consequence of freedom. In itself, freedom is neither good nor evil: it involves a choice of one or the other. Svidrigailov's freedom, the 'liberty' propounded by Western philosophy, political economy and socialist theory as an absolute good, is a false one—in it he reveals himself to be at the mercy of his own animal instincts: without God he is a slave to the impersonal forces of nature, and his personality shrivels and dies. Sonya, on the other hand, who has accepted the necessity and inevitability of suffering, exists in true freedom—she is equally aware of the possibilities for destruction and creation that exist around her, and would concur with Berdyaev's dictum that 'the existence of evil is a proof of God's existence. If the world consisted solely and exclusively of goodness and justice, God would not be necessary, for then the world itself would be God. God exists because evil exists. And this means that God exists because freedom exists.' It is towards this freedom that Raskolnikov makes his way through the pages of *Crime and Punishment* and the swirling alternations of night and day, dream and waking, timelessness and time. His dreams disclose to him the possibilities that hang in the balance: *everything* may be lost, as in the nightmare of the flogged horse, which stands for his own denied self, or *everything* may be gained, as in the fantasy of the Egyptian oasis, where he drinks the water of life:

> A caravan was resting, the camels were lying down peacefully; all around there were palm trees, an entire circle of them; everyone was eating their evening meal. He, however, kept drinking water, straight from the spring that flowed murmuring right by his side. It was so cool, and the water was so wonder-

fully, wonderfully cold and blue, hurrying over various-coloured stones and sand that was so pure, with spangles of gold . . .

Raskolnikov, far from being a madman or psychopathic outcast, is an image of Everyman. His pilgrimage towards salvation is chronicled by Dostoyevsky in terms of the biblical myth of original sin—he has fallen from grace, and must regain it. In his own knowledge of the sacredness of his own person, and of the violation of that sacredness inherent in his crime, he bears within him the seeds of a new life which grows out of the conflict of 'for' and 'against'. The entire 'detective story' form of the novel is intended to simulate the circumstances of an inquisition. Porfiry Petrovich, Zamyotov and the rest of the police apparatus are concerned in the first instance to probe Raskolnikov's soul and to make him aware that the crime he has committed is a sin against the divine presence within himself. Raskolnikov feels little remorse for having killed the old woman, but suffers under a crushing, life-destroying weight of misery at what he has 'done to himself', to use Sonya's words.

One aspect of Raskolnikov's revolt against God that has sometimes been neglected by critics is to be seen in his name: the *Raskol,* or 'Schism', is the term used to describe the split that took place in the Russian Orthodox Church in the mid seventeenth century, when certain liturgical reforms were introduced by Patriarch Nikon. The *raskol 'niki* were sectarians who clung to the old rituals, putting themselves at variance with the civil and ecclesiastical authorities, with whom they came into violent and sometimes bloody conflict. Dostoyevsky had met these 'Old Believers' and their descendants in the labour camp at Omsk, and wrote about them in *The House of the Dead.* In an essay on the Schism, V. S. Solovyov characterized it as a form of 'Russian Protestantism', a disease of true Christianity, diagnosing its central error as a tendency to confuse the human with the divine, the temporal with the eternal, the particular with the universal; denying the supremacy of Christianity's collective principle and reality, the Church, it tended towards a divinization of the individual:

> Containing within it a germ of Protestantism, the Russian Schism cultivated it to its limits. Even among the Old Believers, the true preserver of the ancient heritage and tradition is the individual

person. This person does not live in the past, but in the present; the adopted tradition, here shorn of an advantage over the individual in terms of living wholeness or catholicity (as in the Universal Church) and being in itself no more than a dead formality, is revitalized and reanimated merely by the faith and devoutness of its true preserver—the individual person. No sooner, however, does a position of this kind start to be aware that the centre of gravity is shifting from the dead past to the living present, than the conventional objects of tradition lose all value, and all significance is transferred to the independent, individual bearer of that tradition; from this there proceeds the direct transition to those free sects which notoriously claim personal inspiration and personal righteousness as the basis of religion.

In *Crime and Punishment* there are clear indications that Dostoyevsky intends the reader to associate Raskolnikov with the religious heresy of *staroobryadchestvo* ('Old Ritualism'), not in any specific sense but rather in a general one. In Chapter II of Part Six the investigator Porfiry Petrovich tells Raskolnikov that Mikolka, who has 'confessed' to the crime, comes from a family in which there are 'Runners'—sectarians who travelled around the country begging, and in search of any chance to humble themselves:

> 'And did you know that he's a Raskolnik—or rather, not so much a Raskolnik as simply a sectarian; there were "Runners" in his family, and it's not so long ago since he himself spent two whole years in the country under the spiritual guidance of some elder or other . . . Have you any conception, Rodion Romanovich, of what the word "suffering" means to some of them? They don't do it for the sake of anyone in particular, but just for its own sake, purely and simply as "suffering"; all that matters is to accept suffering, and if it's from the powers-that-be, that's all to the good . . .'

Porfiry's implication, skilfully presented by means of psychological suggestion and interrogation techniques, is that Raskolnikov, too, has been treading this path—and that he must continue to do so if he is eventually to find salvation. For this is one of the main reasons why Raskolnikov is able to be saved from the error into which he has fallen—his illness is of a specifically Russian kind, caused not only by the influence of 'nihilistic' Western ideas, but also by an inborn *raskol 'nichestvo,* an ancient Russian sympathy for and identification with the strong dissenter who challenges the authority of Church and State alike. The Epilogue to the novel describes the beginning of his journey back to them, a journey that will ultimately involve not only his own personal recovery and transformation, but also the regeneration and renewal of Russian society. It is the persistent tracing of this theme of a 'Russian sickness' of spiritual origin and its cure throughout the book that justifies the author's characterization of it as an 'Orthodox novel'.

—David McDuff, "Introduction," *Crime and Punishment* by Fyodor Dostoevsky (New York: Viking, 1991), pp. 25–27

❖

HARRIET MURAV ON RASKOLNIKOV AND HIS ENVIRONMENT

[Harriet Murav (b. 1955), a professor in the department of German and Russian at the University of California at Davis, has written *Holy Foolishness: Dostoevsky's Novels and the Poetics of Cultural Critique* (1992), from which the following extract is taken. Here, Murav probes Raskolnikov's actions in light of the changing theories of criminal behavior and the effect of environment on the criminal.]

One offshoot of this new scientific discourse was the notion that crime is a protest against a victimizing environment. We hear about this idea during a conversation among Raskolnikov, Razumikhin, his bumbling but well-intentioned friend, and the court investigator, Porfirii Petrovich. Razumikhin explains that the view of the socialists is that "crime is a protest against the abnormality of the social structure—and only that and nothing more." Razumikhin says that the socialists hoped to solve all of mankind's problems by leaping over "living history" in order to arrive at a mathematically perfect solution, which he character-izes as nothing more than the correct arrangements of the cor-ridors and rooms in the phalansteries—a reference to the communal living arrangements designed by the utopian social-ist and mathematician Charles Fourier.

As a member of the Petrashevskii circle in the 1840's, Dostoevsky had become familiar with the ideas of Fourier and his disciples. He had also no doubt become familiar with Butashevich-Petrashevskii's *Pocket Dictionary of Foreign Words,* a radical philosophical tract in the form of a dictionary, published in 1845 and 1846. The entry for "the normal condition" (*normal'noe sostoianie*) contains a whole treatise about the relation between the individual and the environment and the need to reconstruct society along more "normal lines." In this little treatise, and in Razumikhin's use of the term "abnormality," we see the way in which the language of disease has become assimilated into moral and political discourse.

Petrashevskii wrote that in "the most recent philosophical theories," the normal condition is a technical term that signifies "the normality of the development of society and mankind." His conception of a "normally developed individual" is one in whom all the passions are "harmoniously developed" (*Karmannyi slovar' inostrannykh slov*). The notion of the harmonious reconciliation of the passions and of their importance for the "normal condition" of the individual is derived from Fourier, who saw in human passion a force akin to the universal, nonorganic force of attraction, that is, gravity. In *Crime and Punishment,* it is the medical student Zametin who remarks to Raskolnikov's sister that there are very few "harmonious individuals in the world."

Petrashevskii goes on to say that such normal development depends less on the individual than on society, which must provide him with the minimum necessary for his existence. The normal condition can be said to have been achieved only when "the spirit of unity pervades; and everything that is considered oppressive and repulsive is transformed into a source of the immediate enjoyment of life." For Petrashevskii, the normal condition is an ideal one, in which both the individual and society are in a state of harmony. Once society is reconstructed normally, all the sources of conflict, both internal (the struggle between reason and passion) and external (the conflicts between various members of society) will be removed, and unity will be achieved. The reform of human nature is to be brought about by the reorganization of society as a whole. In

Crime and Punishment, Fourier is quoted only to be parodied. Lebeziatnikov says that Sonia Marmeladova's prostitution is a protest against "the structure of society."

In *Crime and Punishment,* the veiled reference to Petrashevskii and Fourier serves more than one purpose. The debate about crime and the environment is a prologue to the deadly cat-and-mouse game between Porfirii Petrovich and Raskolnikov, of which Razumikhin is completely unaware. Porfirii professes interest in Raskolnikov's ideas about crime, which he has read about in an article that Raskolnikov has published. For Raskolnikov, crime is not merely a form of social protest, as it was for Lacenaire. As Porfirii tells us, Raskolnikov believes that society can be divided into two classes, the "ordinary" and the "extraordinary." The extraordinary, the class of supermen, have the capacity "to utter their *new word"* and therefore have the right to commit crimes. Porfirii Petrovich playfully suggests that Raskolnikov counts himself as such a superman.

By the time Dostoevsky completed *Crime and Punishment,* the study of the social environment had gone beyond Fourier. We have spoken of the way statistics provided a new basis for evaluating behavior. N. Nekliudov's *Criminal Statistical Studies* (1865), for example, examined the physiological significance of the age of the "human organism" in relation to crime. The name for this new theory was "moral statistics," or, alternatively, "social physics." In *Crime and Punishment,* Dostoevsky reflects on the implications of "moral statistics" indirectly, relying, as we will see, on Raskolnikov's "word."

—Harriet Murav, *Holy Foolishness: Dostoevsky's Novels and the Poetics of Cultural Critique* (Stanford: Stanford University Press, 1992), pp. 53–55

❖

DAVID MATUEL ON THE EPILOGUE OF *CRIME AND PUNISHMENT*

[David Matuel is a professor of modern languages at Wright State University. In this extract, Matuel counters the arguments that the epilogue of *Crime and*

Punishment is unsatisfactory and that it presents
Raskolnikov out of character.]

A close examination of the epilogue and the rest of the novel
⟨. . .⟩ reveals that the connections between the two are numerous and pervasive both in a psychological and in an aesthetic
sense. There is no reason to believe that in the end Raskolnikov
rises to new life spontaneously and without warning. Meier-
Graefe's argument to the contrary notwithstanding, there is a
wealth of biographical data indicating that the hero is psychologically capable of the extraordinary events that begin in the
epilogue. In fact, the possibility of his conversion should be
obvious to those who read carefully and without prejudice,
allowing themselves to be persuaded by the tendency of
Dostoevsky's thought and by the numerous clues that point to
the inevitability of a happy conclusion. While it is true that
some of the positive events and actions in the hero's life can be
interpreted in more than one way (as is so often the case with
Dostoevsky), it is also true that much of this material does not
admit of ambiguity at all and contributes mightily to the plausi-
bility of the ending.

Raskolnikov's relationships with other people provide the
principal psychological evidence that despite his conceit and
his exaggerated self-consciousness he is nevertheless able to
accept Sonia's love and guidance and thus begin the long spiritual journey she exhorts him to make. Robert Louis Jackson has
emphasized the fact that in his dealings with others
Raskolnikov's behavior passes through two distinct and seemingly contradictory phases, the one quickly succeeding the
other: first, he shows a profound sympathy toward those in
need and takes immediate steps to alleviate their suffering;
afterwards he feels disgust with himself for having betrayed his
intellectual principles. Though strongly opposed to each other,
these two aspects of his behavior are nevertheless equally gen-
uine and worthy of any critic's serious consideration. Until
recently far too much attention has been given to the second
aspect while the first has been largely ignored. Yet Razumikhin,
Raskolnikov's only friend and the one who knows him as well
as anyone can, speaks of "two opposite personalities" in his
friend. On the one hand he is "generous and kind;" on the
other, "cold and unfeeling." We see the more human

Raskolnikov in the second chapter of Part One, when he experiences an inexplicable urge to mingle with people after a long period of self-imposed isolation. This pattern is repeated several times in the novel. Often enough his attempts to reestablish contact with the world around him end with a concrete act of charity. Thus he gives twenty copecks to a policeman for the care of a young girl who is harassed by a lecherous middle-aged man. He gives five copecks to a street singer and an organ-grinder. He is very solicitous of Marmeladov and later helps defray the cost of his funeral. He defends Sonia from Luzhin's machinations during the funeral repast and exposes him as a contemptible liar. After confessing his crime, he embraces Sonia and weeps. During his trial we discover that he once supported a sick and impoverished fellow student for six months and that after his friend's death he showed himself equally generous toward the bereaved father. When the father also died, he paid the burial expenses. In addition to all this, he once risked his own life to save two children from a burning building. His sense of compassion, which has been an integral part of his personality since childhood and which is manifested from time to time throughout the novel, is undeniable. It endows his actions with a magnanimity that runs counter to the malevolence of his scheme and the cruelty of his crime.

Before he commits the murder, Raskolnikov's thoughts reflect a curious ambivalence that suggests a certain disenchantment with his plan and even a desire to be delivered from it. After making a trial visit to the pawnbroker in the very first chapter, he feels a profound repugnance. At that moment and at various other times as well he is horrified by the thought of what he intends to do. In his first dream he sees a horse flogged to death by its drunken owner and is appalled by the realization that he will kill the old woman in the same way. As the time of the murder approaches, he begs God to show him how to renounce his plan forever. Still, the plan is carried out and the pawnbroker is brutally killed. She is not the only victim, however. Her childlike half sister Lizaveta returns to the apartment unexpectedly, and Raskolnikov is forced to kill her, too. After this unexpected turn in his fortunes he feels a compelling need to run to the police station and confess his crime. This he does not do, of course, until the end of the novel. Nevertheless, the fact that he leaves so many incriminating traces of his guilt and behaves in a way that arouses suspicion suggests not only that he is willing to turn himself in to the authorities but that he positively *wants* to be caught. Several critics have explained this desire in terms of Raskolnikov's scheme, claiming that by accepting the punishment for his crime he shows that he is truly one of the "great men" of history, whose suffering is often commensurate with their greatness. Yet it is also possible that in drawing the attention of the police to himself he is seeking a kind of spiritual purgation and renewal much like his thematic double, the peasant Mikolka, who confesses to a crime he has not committed in order to assume the burden of expiation. Maurice Beebe has even suggested that "the ending [of the novel] is artistically and psychologically inevitable because the basic motive of regeneration is the same as the underlying motive for the crime," and that motive, in his view, is the desire to suffer.

Raskolnikov is emphatically not bereft of lofty sentiments, nor does he lack the capacity to change. The most impressive and perhaps least often adduced evidence for this is the abundance of references to his childhood. The theme of childhood is vitally important in the mature Dostoevsky, and *Crime and Punishment* is, among many other things, a novel about children—their degradation, the profanation of their innocence, and the saving power of their presence. We find them throughout the book: in the grimy streets, in the crowded little apartments, and even in the dreams of the principal characters. Raskolnikov's recollections of his own childhood highlight the noble but long suppressed elements of his personality which come to full fruition only in the epilogue. Mention is first made of them at the end of the long letter he receives from his mother, who implores him to recall how he used to pray when his father was still alive. Further reference is made to Raskolnikov's early piety in his first dream. There we see him as a seven-year old boy walking to the cemetery with his father. In a prefatory remark the narrator observes that the boy loved the cemetery church and the old priest who served there. As the events of the dream unfold the child is moved to pity at the sight of the horse dying under the blows of its master and his friends. His pity is mixed with anger as he rushes to strike at

those who have committed this barbarous act, which symbolically parallels the act that he himself will commit as an adult.
Even after he murders the pawnbroker and her sister, he is
haunted by reminiscences of his boyhood piety. In a series of
apparently disconnected dreams and musings he recalls a
church and the ringing of bells on a Sunday morning. It may
well be the very church of which he was so fond as a child.

—David Matuel, "In Defense of the Epilogue of *Crime and
Punishment*," *Studies in the Novel* 24, No. 1 (Spring 1992):
27–29

❖

ALBA AMOIA ON RASKOLNIKOV'S CONSCIENCE

[Alba Amoia (b. 1928) has been a professor at
Columbia University and Hunter College of the City
University of New York. She is the author of *Albert
Camus* (1989), *Thomas Mann's Fiorenza* (1990), and
Feodor Dostoevsky (1993), from which the following
extract is taken. Here, Amoia maintains that
Raskolnikov sees his crime as a rational and logical act
but then deteriorates into endless self-analysis and
moral brooding.]

To escape from his social and economic limitations and attain a
position in which he can exercise the talent he is sure he pos-
sesses, Raskolnikov conceives and carries out what has been
called a "philosophical crime," the hatchet murder of a "use-
less, even harmful" old woman who lends money at usurious
rates—and whom Raskolnikov has privately condemned to
death on what he considers unanswerable intellectual grounds.
In addition, he impulsively commits a second murder of a
purely expedient character, using his hatchet to split the skull
of the woman's half-witted sister when she inadvertently enters
the room where her sister has just been murdered. In the wake
of this all too vividly described murder, Raskolnikov himself is
seized with feelings of "horror and disgust"—a leitmotiv of the
novel. For the time being, however, he neither repents nor considers himself a criminal.

As the implications of the deed unfold in his conscience over the following weeks, Raskolnikov at first attempts to justify his action as a "rational" crime, committed in "an act of boldness" by an "exceptional man." "One must have the courage to dare"; "I wanted to become a Napoleon"; "I wanted to find out whether . . . I am some trembling vermin or whether I have the *right*"—these are some of the well-known descriptions of his attitude, uttered by himself in the course of his later confession.

Much of the novel is taken up with a process of self-analysis in the course of which Raskolnikov, this nineteenth-century "superman," gradually reveals the nature of his own motivations. Some of these he had already put forward in a published article in which he had stressed a supposed distinction between "ordinary" and "exceptional" human beings. A member of the latter group, Raskolnikov contends, has "a right . . . to permit conscience to step over certain obstacles . . . if it is absolutely necessary for the fulfillment of his ideas on which . . . the welfare of all mankind may depend." Such figures as Lycurgus, Solon, Mahomet, and Napoleon, according to Raskolnikov, had been superior benefactors, lawgivers, and arbiters of mankind; and each of them had shed rivers of blood promulgating new laws for a new world order. He, too, Raskolnikov indicated, had determined to commit an act of hubris or moral presumption in order to take his place among humanity's proud exceptions.

Raskolnikov is highly knowledgeable, well-read, and intelligent, as well as courageous; but his almost insane vanity is incompatible with normal social behavior. Ragged, unshaven, and tousled, he is uncommunicative and solitary and wears a fixed expression of haughtiness and arrogant mockery. Mankind fills him with existential nausea—"a sort of infinite, almost physical feeling of disgust with everything he came across—malevolent, obstinate, virulent. He hated the people he met in the street, he hated their faces, the way they walked, the way they moved. If any man had addressed him now, he would have spat on him or perhaps even bitten him."

And yet despite his strange silence—a silence that, in Bernard Shaw's words, is "the most perfect expression of scorn"—Raskolnikov considers himself an idealist who is concerned about the betterment of "all suffering humanity." Deep within his hardened heart he cherishes his family; indeed, one of the original motivations for his crime was the desire to help his mother and sister in their personal predicament. In some ways one is reminded of Dostoevsky himself, who at times preferred to be cruel rather than put his real feelings into words. "I have such a vile, repulsive character," he once wrote Mikhail, "sometimes when my heart is swimming in love you can't get a tender word from me."

Raskolnikov's heart and mind, indeed, seem almost to operate in separate, watertight compartments. His one friend, the warmhearted Razumikhin—a character most certainly modeled on Mikhail Dostoevsky—observes that Raskolnikov, hiding his real feelings, sometimes becomes cold and inhumanly callous "just as if there were two people of diametrically opposed characters living in him, each taking charge of him in turn." Seeking "the moral solution" for the crime he is about to commit, Dostoevsky tells the reader, Raskolnikov "could no longer find any conscious objections to his plans *in his mind.* But *at heart* he never really took himself seriously, and he went on . . . fumbling for some valid objections . . . *as though someone were compelling and pushing him to do it*" (italics added).

This innate duality defeats Raskolnikov's attempts to rationalize his actions after the murders have been committed. He vacillates between supreme vanity and humble submissiveness, and only later will his conscience enter into the analysis of the sorrow he has brought upon himself. "Whoever has a conscience will no doubt suffer, if he realizes his mistake," he reflects. "That's his punishment—on top of penal servitude. . . . Let him suffer, if he is sorry for his victim. Suffering and pain are always necessary for men of great sensibility and deep feeling. Really great men, it seems to me, must feel great sorrow on earth." Accused of having turned his face from God, Raskolnikov will readily concede that it was Satan who had tempted him and goaded him into committing the crime: "It was the devil who killed the old hag, not I."

—Alba Amoia, *Feodor Dostoevsky* (New York: Continuum, 1993), pp. 53–55

❖

Books by
Fyodor Dostoevsky

Russian text:

Bednye lyudi ⟨*Poor Folk*⟩. 1846.

Dvoinik ⟨*The Double*⟩. 1846.

Netochka Nezvanova. 1849.

Dyadyushkin son ⟨*Uncle's Dream*⟩. 1859.

Selo Stepanchikovo ⟨*The Friend of the Family*⟩. 1859.

Zapiski iz mertvogo doma ⟨*The House of the Dead*⟩. 1860–62.

Unizhennye i oskorblennye ⟨*The Insulted and Injured*⟩. 1861.

Prestuplenie i nakazanie ⟨*Crime and Punishment*⟩. 1866.

Igrok ⟨*The Gambler*⟩. 1867.

Idiot ⟨*The Idiot*⟩. 1868.

Vechnyi muzh ⟨*The Eternal Husband*⟩. 1870.

Besy ⟨*The Possessed*⟩. 1872.

Podrostok ⟨*A Raw Youth*⟩. 1875.

Brat'ya Karamazov ⟨*The Brothers Karamazov*⟩. 1880.

Polnoe sobranie khudozhestvennykh proizvedenii ⟨*Collected Works*⟩. Ed. B. Tomashevskii and K. Khalabaev. 1926–30. 13 vols.

Pis'ma ⟨*Letters*⟩. Ed. A. S. Dolinin. 1928–59. 4 vols.

Polnoe sobranie sochinenii ⟨*Collected Works*⟩. Ed. G. M. Fridlender et al. 1972–90. 30 vols.

English translations:

Buried Alive; or, Ten Years of Penal Servitude in Siberia ⟨*The House of the Dead*⟩. Tr. Marie von Thilo. 1881.

Crime and Punishment. Tr. Frederick Whishaw. 1886.

Injury and Insult. Tr. Frederick Whishaw. 1886.

The Friend of the Family and The Gambler. Tr. Frederick Whishaw. 1887.

The Idiot. Tr. Frederick Whishaw. 1887.

Uncle's Dream and The Permanent Husband. Tr. Frederick Whishaw. 1888.

Poor Folk. Tr. Lena Milman. 1894.

The Brothers Karamazov. Tr. Constance Garnett. 1912.

The Idiot. Tr. Constance Garnett. 1913.

The Possessed. Tr. Constance Garnett. 1913.

Letters from the Underworld. Tr. C. J. Hogarth. 1913.

Crime and Punishment. Tr. Constance Garnett. 1914.

The Insulted and Injured. Tr. Constance Garnett. 1914.

The House of the Dead. Tr. Constance Garnett. 1915.

Pages from the Journal of an Author. Tr. S. S. Koteliansky and J. Middleton Murry. 1916.

A Raw Youth. Tr. Constance Garnett. 1916.

The Eternal Husband and Other Stories. Tr. Constance Garnett. 1917.

The Gambler and Other Stories. Tr. Constance Garnett. 1917.

White Nights and Other Stories. Tr. Constance Garnett. 1918.

An Honest Thief and Other Stories. Tr. Constance Garnett. 1919.

The Friend of the Family. Tr. Constance Garnett. 1920.

Stavrogin's Confession and the Plan of The Life of a Great Sinner. Tr. S. S. Koteliansky and Virginia Woolf. 1922.

Letters and Reminiscences. Tr. S. S. Koteliansky and J. Middleton Murry. 1923.

New Dostoevsky Letters. Tr. S. S. Koteliansky. 1929.

Letters to His Wife. Tr. Elizabeth Hill and Doris Mudie. 1930.

The Diary of a Writer. Tr. Boris Brasol. 1949.

Crime and Punishment. Tr. David Magarshack. 1951.

Crime and Punishment. Tr. Jessie Coulson. 1953.

The Devils ⟨The Possessed⟩. Tr. David Magarshack. 1953.

Best Short Stories. Tr. David Magarshack. 1955.

The Idiot. Tr. David Magarshack. 1955.

Summer Impressions. Tr. Kyril Fitzlyon. 1955.

Winter Notes on Summer Impressions. Tr. Richard Lee Renfield. 1955.

Dostoevsky: A Self-Portrait. Tr. Jessie Coulson. 1962.

The Possessed. Tr. Andrew R. MacAndrew. 1962.

The Notebooks for The Idiot. Ed. Edward Wasiolek. Tr. Katherine Strelsky. 1967.

The Notebooks for Crime and Punishment. Ed. and tr. Edward Wasiolek. 1967.

The Notebooks for The Possessed. Ed. Edward Wasiolek. Tr. Victor Terras. 1968.

Notes from Underground. Ed. Robert G. Durgy. Tr. Serge Shishkoff. 1969.

The Notebooks for A Raw Youth. Ed. Edward Wasiolek. Tr. Victor Terras. 1969.

Netochka Nezvanova. Tr. Ann Dunnigan. 1970.

The Adolescent. Tr. Andrew R. MacAndrew. 1971.

The Gambler. Tr. Victor Terras. 1972.

The Unpublished Dostoevsky: Diaries and Notebooks (1860–81). Ed. Carl R. Proffer. Tr. T. S. Berczynski et al. 1973–76. 3 vols.

Notes from Underground; The Double. Tr. Jessie Coulson. 1972.

Notes from Underground. Tr. Andrew R. MacAndrew. 1980.

Memoirs from the House of the Dead. Tr. Jessie Coulson. 1983.

The Village of Stepanchikovo and Its Inhabitants: From the Notes of an Unknown. Tr. Ignat Avsey. 1983.

The Double: Two Versions. Tr. Evelyn Harden. 1985.

The Crocodile. Tr. S. D. Cioran. 1985.

Selected Letters. Ed. Joseph Frank and David I. Goldstein. Tr. Andrew R. MacAndrew. 1987.

Poor Folk and Other Stories. Tr. David McDuff. 1988.

Complete Letters. Ed. and tr. David Lowe and Ronald Meyer. 1988–91. 5 vols.

Notes from Underground. Tr. Michael R. Katz. 1989.

The Brothers Karamazov. Tr. Richard Pevear and Larissa Volokhonsky. 1990.

Crime and Punishment. Tr. David McDuff. 1991.

Notes from the Underground and The Gambler. Tr. Jane Kentish. 1991.

Crime and Punishment. Tr. Richard Pevear and Larissa Volokhonsky. 1992.

The Idiot. Tr. Alan Myers. 1992.

Devils ⟨The Possessed⟩. Tr. Michael R. Katz. 1992.

Notes from Underground. Tr. Richard Pevear and Larissa
Volokhonsky. 1993.

A Writer's Diary. Tr. Kenneth Lantz. 1993–94. 2 vols.

Demons ⟨The Possessed⟩. Tr. Richard Pevear and Larissa
Volokhonsky. 1994.

An Accidental Family. Tr. Michael Freeborn. 1994.

The Brothers Karamazov. Tr. Ignat Avsey. 1994.

Works about Fyodor Dostoevsky and Crime and Punishment

Anderson, Roger B. "*Crime and Punishment:* Psychomyth and the Making of a Hero." *Canadian-American Slavic Studies* 11 (1977): 523–28.

Bakhtin, Mikhail. *Problems of Dostoevsky's Poetics.* Tr. Caryl Emerson. Minneapolis: University of Minnesota Press, 1984.

Bloom, Harold, ed. *Fyodor Dostoevsky's* Crime and Punishment. New York: Chelsea House, 1988.

Breger, Louis. *Dostoevsky: The Author as Psychoanalyst.* New York: New York University Press, 1989.

Brown, Nathalie Babel. *Hugo and Dostoevsky.* Ann Arbor, MI: Ardis, 1978.

Burnett, Leon, ed. *F. M. Dostoevsky (1821–1881): A Centenary Collection.* Colchester, UK: University of Essex, 1981.

Cassedy, Steven. "The Formal Problem of the Epilogue in *Crime and Punishment:* The Logic of Tragic and Christian Structures." *Dostoevsky Studies* 3 (1982): 171–89.

Catteau, Jacques. *Dostoyevsky and the Process of Literary Creation.* Tr. Audrey Littlewood. Cambridge: Cambridge University Press, 1989.

Cox, Gary. *Tyrant and Victim in Dostoevsky.* Columbus, OH: Slavica, 1984.

Dilman, Ilham. "Dostoyevsky: Psychology and the Novelist." In *Philosophy and Literature,* ed. A. Phillips Griffiths. Cambridge: Cambridge University Press, 1984, pp. 95–114.

Discherl, Denis. *Dostoevsky and the Catholic Church.* Chicago: Loyola University Press, 1986.

Dowler, Wayne. *Dostoevsky, Grigorov, and Native Soil Conservatism.* Toronto: University of Toronto Press, 1982.

Frank, Joseph. *Dostoevsky: The Seeds of Revolt 1821–1849*. Princeton: Princeton University Press, 1976.

———. *Dostoevsky: The Years of Ordeal 1850–1859*. Princeton: Princeton University Press, 1983.

———. *Dostoevsky: The Stir of Liberation 1860–1865*. Princeton: Princeton University Press, 1986.

———. *Dostoevsky: The Miraculous Years 1865–1871*. Princeton: Princeton University Press, 1995.

———. "The Genesis of *Crime and Punishment*." In *Russianness: Studies on a Nation's Identity,* ed. Robert L. Belknap. Ann Arbor, MI: Ardis, 1990, pp. 124–43.

Goldstein, David I. *Dostoevsky and the Jews*. Austin: University of Texas Press, 1981.

Holk, Andre van. "Moral Themes in Dostoevsky's *Crime and Punishment*." *Essays in Poetics* 14 (1989): 28–75.

Holquist, Michael. *Dostoevsky and the Novel*. Princeton: Princeton University Press, 1977.

Ivanits, Linda. "Suicide and Folk Belief in *Crime and Punishment*." In *The Golden Age of Russian Literature and Thought,* ed. Derek Offord. New York: St. Martin's Press, 1992, pp. 138–48.

Jackson, Robert Louis. *Dialogues with Dostoevsky: The Overwhelming Questions*. Stanford: Stanford University Press, 1993.

Jones, Malcolm V. *Dostoyevsky After Bakhtin: Readings in Dostoyevsky's Fantastic Realism*. Cambridge: Cambridge University Press, 1990.

Jones, Malcolm V., and Garth M. Terry, ed. *New Essays on Dostoyevsky*. Cambridge: Cambridge University Press, 1983.

Kanow, David K. *The Dialogic Sign: Essays on the Major Novels of Dostoevsky*. New York: Peter Lang, 1991.

Karyakin, Yuri. *Rereading Dostoevsky*. Tr. S. Chulaki. Moscow: Novosti Press, 1971.

Kiremidjian, David. "*Crime and Punishment:* Matricide and the Woman Question." *American Imago* 33 (1976): 403–33.

Kjetisaa, Geer. *Fyodor Dostoyevsky: A Writer's Life.* Tr. Siri Hustvedt and David McDuff. New York: Viking, 1987.

Kraeger, Linda, and Joe Barnhart. *Dostoevsky on Evil and Atonement.* Lewiston, NY: Edwin Mellen Press, 1992.

MacGregor, Catherine. " 'Especially Pictures of Families': Alcoholism, Codependency, and *Crime and Punishment.*" *Dionysos* 3, No. 2 (Fall 1991): 3–20.

Miller, Robin Feur, ed. *Critical Essays on Dostoevsky.* Boston: G. K. Hall, 1986.

Mitchell, Giles. "Pathological Narcissism and Violence in Dostoevskii's Svidrigailov." *Canadian-American Slavic Studies* 24 (1990): 1–18.

Morson, Gary Saul. "How to Read *Crime and Punishment.*" *Commentary* 93, No. 6 (June 1992): 49–53.

Panichas, George A. *The Burden of Vision: Dostoevsky's Spiritual Art.* Chicago: Gateway, 1985.

Rice, James L. *Dostoevsky and the Healing Art.* Ann Arbor, MI: Ardis, 1985.

Rowe, W. W. "Dostoevskian Patterned Antinomy and Its Function in *Crime and Punishment.*" *Slavic and East European Journal* 16 (1972): 287–96.

Seduro, Vladimir. *Dostoevsky in Russian Literary Criticism 1846–1956.* New York: Octagon, 1969.

Shaw, J. Thomas. "Raskolnikov's Dreams." *Slavic and East European Journal* 2 (1973): 131–45.

Straus, Nina Pelikan. *Dostoevsky and the Woman Question.* New York: St. Martin's Press, 1994.

Sutherland, Stewart R. "Language and Interpretation in *Crime and Punishment.*" *Philosophy and Literature* 2 (1978): 223–36.

Ugrinsky, Alexej; Lambasa, Frank S.; and Ozolins, Valija K., ed. *Dostoevski and the Human Condition After a Century.* Westport, CT: Greenwood Press, 1986.

Ward, Bruce K. *Dostoyevsky's Critique of the West: The Quest for the Earthly Paradise.* Waterloo, Ontario: Wilfrid Laurier University Press, 1986.

Wasiolek, Edward. *Dostoevsky: The Major Fiction.* Cambridge, MA: MIT Press, 1964.

————, ed. Crime and Punishment *and the Critics.* San Francisco: Wadsworth, 1961.

Welch, Lois M. "Luzhin's Crime and the Advantages of Melodrama in Dostoevsky's *Crime and Punishment.*" *Texas Studies in Literature and Language* 18 (1976): 135–46.

Welleck, René, ed. *Dostoevsky: A Collections of Critical Essays.* Englewood Cliffs, NJ: Prentice-Hall, 1962.

Zdanys, Jonas. "Raskolnikov and Frankenstein: The Deadly Search for a Rational Paradise." *Cithara* 1 (1976): 57–67.

Index of
Themes and Ideas

REPENTANCE, as theme, 18, 19, 20, 22, 23, 26, 32, 35, 38, 73. *See also* Suffering

SONYA, compared to Sofiya Andreevna (*A Raw Youth*), 34; and Raskolnikov, 25–27; and her role in the novel, 10, 11, 12, 15, 17, 18, 19, 20, 21, 22, 23, 32, 35, 50, 51, 65, 70, 72; compared to Darya Shatova (*The Possessed*), 34

SUFFERING, as theme, 13, 16, 18, 20, 32, 34, 67, 73. *See also* Repentance

SVIDRIGAILOV: compared to Yulian Mastokovich (*A Christmas Tree and a Wedding*), 37; compared to Fyodor Pavlovich (*Brothers Karamazov*), 5–46; and his role in the novel, 11, 17, 18, 19, 20–21, 24, 50–51, 65; compared to Prince Valkovski (*The Insulted and Injured*), 37–38; inspired by writings of E.T.A. Hoffman, 36–38

TOLSTOY, LEO, compared to Fyodor Dostoevsky, 33, 63

WHITEJACKET (*White Jacket* [Melville]), as compared to Raskolnikov, 61–63

ZAMETOV, and his role in the novel, 14, 16, 50, 66